Rainforest Watercolor

A COLORING WORKBOOK

Clare Therese Gray

PAGE STREET
PUBLISHING CO.

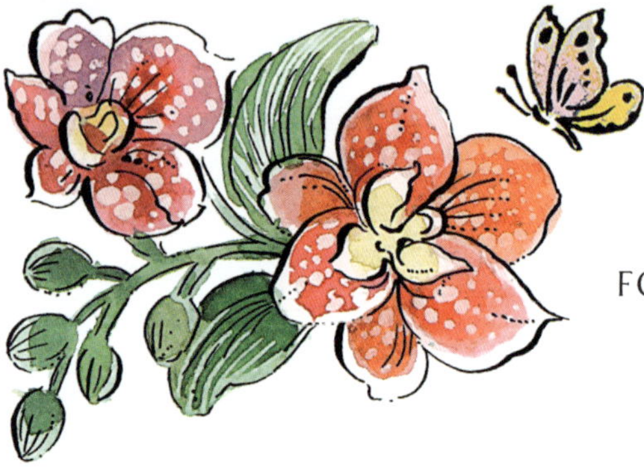

FOR GRACE, TOM, AND BETH,
WITH MY LOVE X

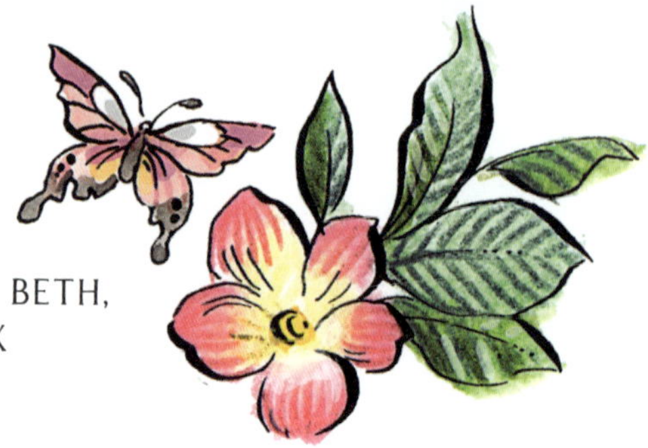

First published in 2025 by
Page Street Publishing Co.
27 Congress Street, Suite 1511
Salem, MA 01970
www.pagestreetpublishing.com

Distributed by Macmillan, sales in Canada by The Canadian Manda Group.

29 28 27 26 25 1 2 3 4 5

ISBN-13: 979-8-89003-346-8

Printed and bound in China

Page Street Publishing protects our planet by donating to nonprofits like The Trustees, which focuses on local land conservation.

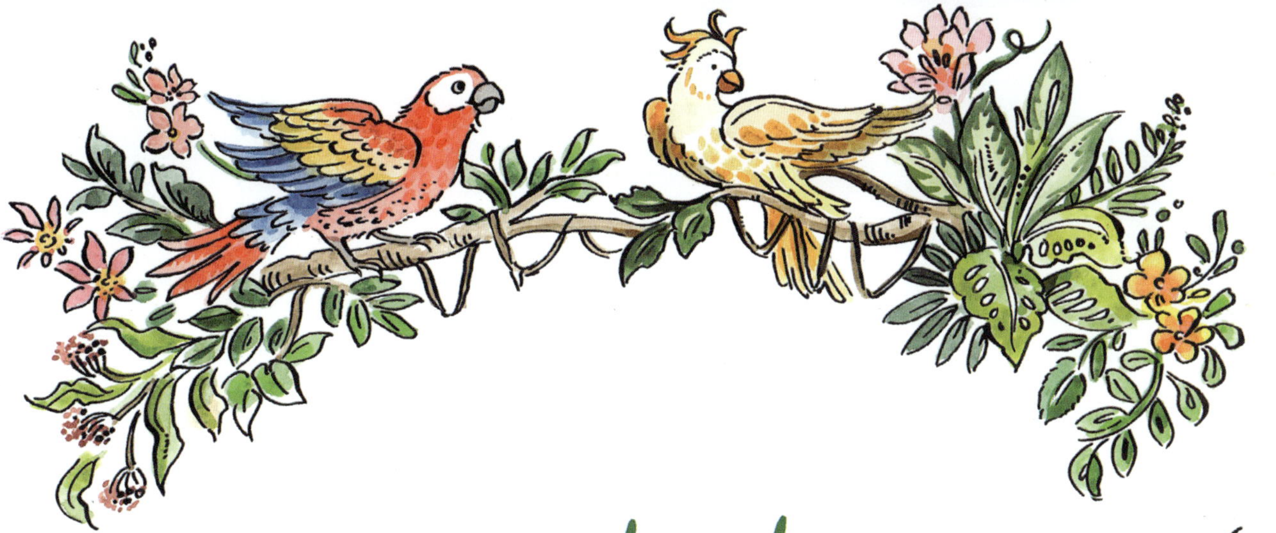

Contents

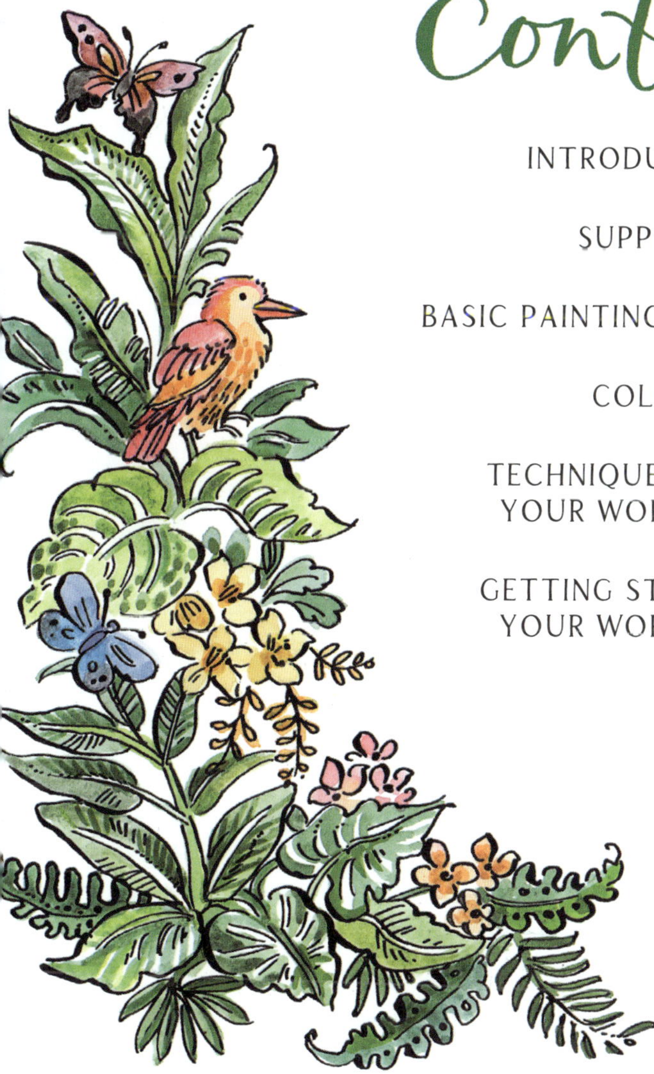

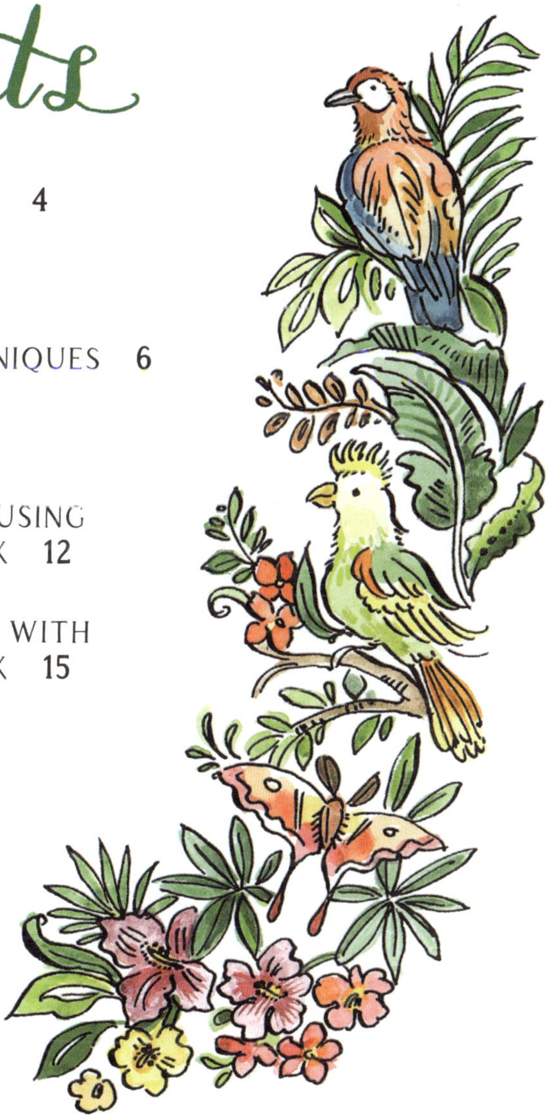

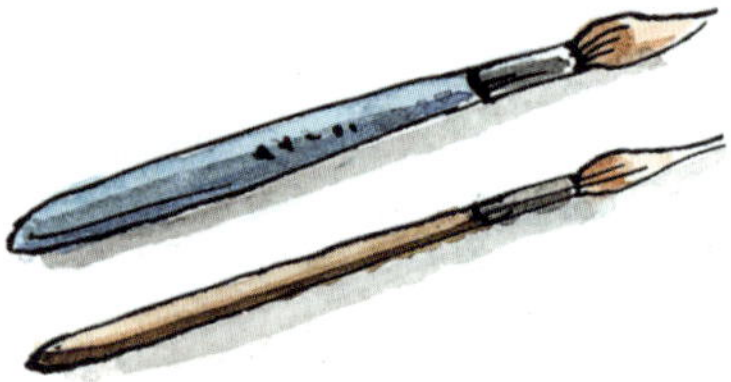

Introduction

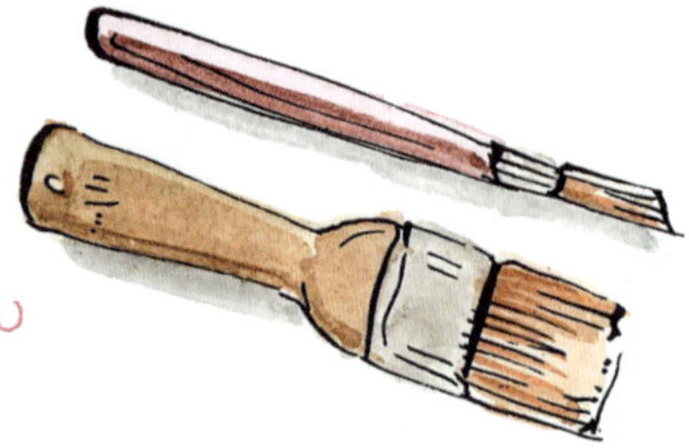

Welcome to *Rainforest Watercolor*, my second watercolor workbook of playful pen and ink drawings ready for you to paint. This coloring book will journey through an imaginative rainforest, from animal portraits to immersive landscapes, exotic tropical birds, and ornate flora and fauna-inspired patterns.

This is your space to develop your personal practice with watercolor, but also to explore color and pattern design. Whether it's the first time that you have picked up a paintbrush or if you're looking for a relaxing space to escape and unleash your creativity, thank you for being here.

This brief introduction is designed to cover the basics of watercolor painting, give you a few useful hints and tips, and kick-start your journey from the very first page. Feel free to pop back and use it as a handy reference for ideas for color mixing, texture, and detailing.

I can't wait to see how you use this book. As always you can find me on Instagram @claretheresegray—please share your work with the hashtag #colorwithclare!

Clare

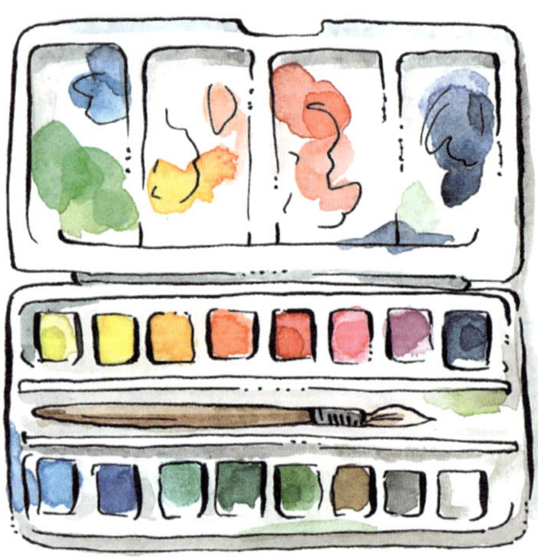

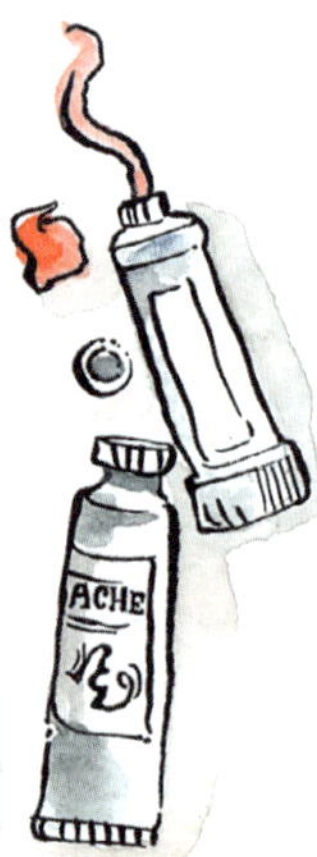

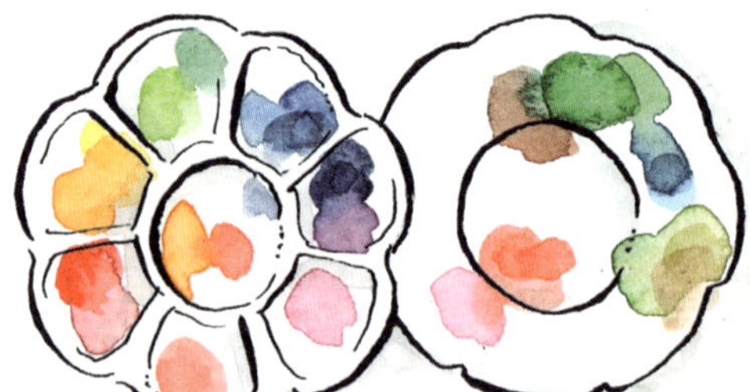

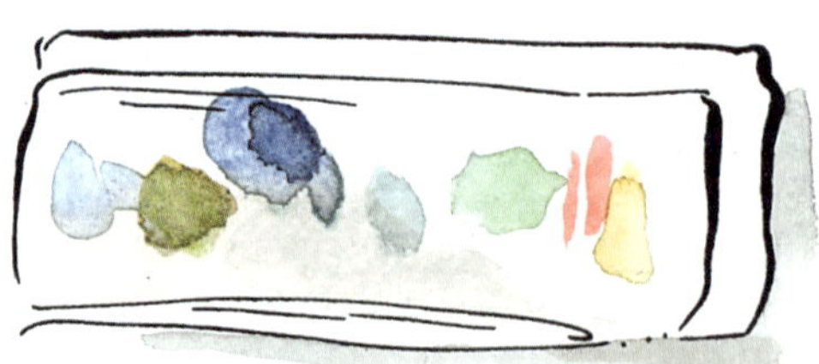

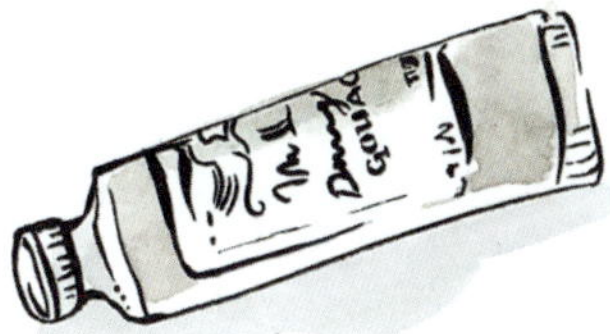

Supplies

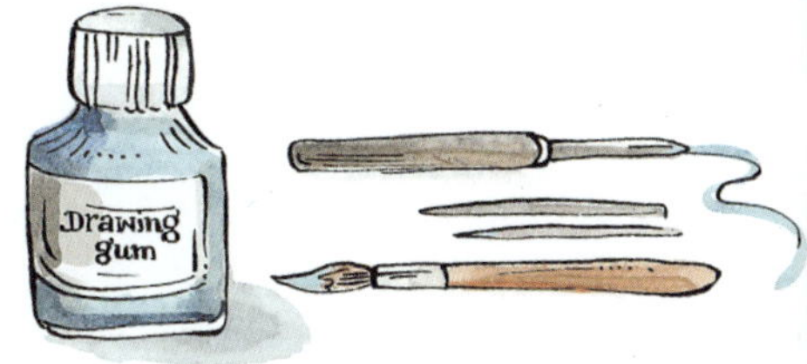

- **Watercolor set:** Watercolors come in small half pans, which are small rectangular "cakes" of dry paint, in 12, 24, and 48+ colors. Watercolor also comes in tubes of wet paint, which you can squeeze into empty pans and then leave to dry to create your own unique set.

- **Brushes:** A few round watercolor brushes (sizes 0–6), a fine brush or two (0–000). I also find a very small angled brush (¼ inch [6 mm]) and a flat wash brush (1 inch [2.5 cm]) useful.

- **Paper towels and palette:** Paper towels are helpful for blotting and cleaning brushes, and a palette is great for mixing color.

- **Small bottle of masking fluid, aka drawing gum, and applicators:** Small bottle of masking fluid, aka drawing gum, and applicators for keeping areas clean and white. You can use an old fine synthetic brush, dip pen, or ruling pen.

- **White gouache:** A small, 14-milliliter tube will suit well.

- **Sketchbook/watercolor paper pad:** The paper in this book is 240 gsm watercolor art paper, which is of medium weight and means that you can add some (but not lots of) water to the page before it starts wrinkling. It's very helpful to have an additional pad of watercolor/cartridge paper for color swatches and experiments.

- **Watercolor pencils:** A variety in both bright and muted shades is useful.

- **Water jars:** Clean jars of water are essential for fresh, bright color. This water needs to be changed frequently and the sides of the jar wiped down to avoid unwanted color mistakes.

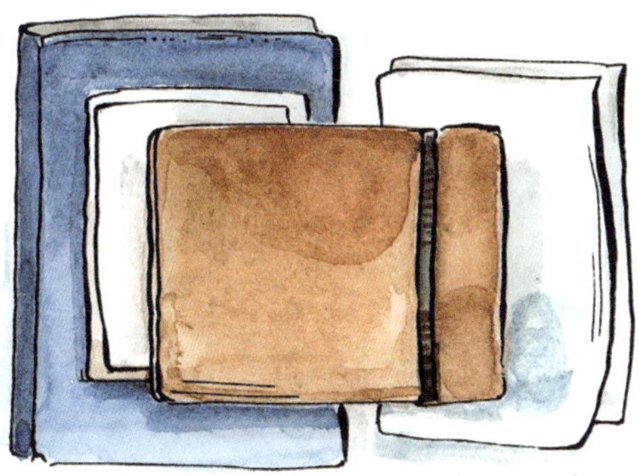

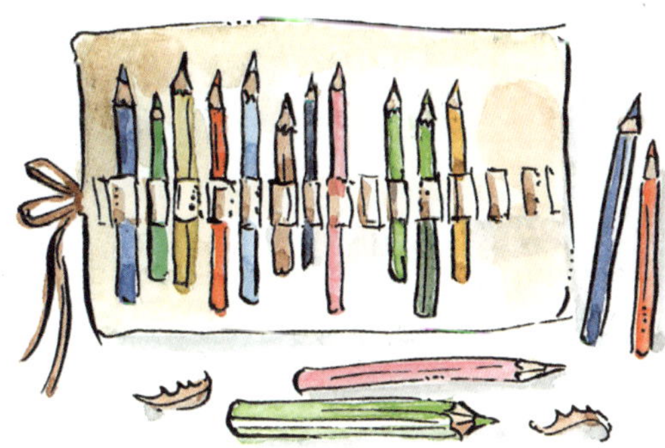

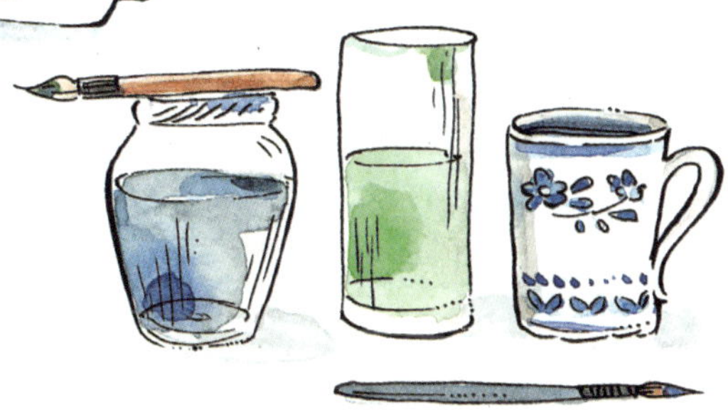

Basic Painting Techniques

Here are a few basic techniques that I hope will be useful if you're new to watercolor.

Make sure you always start with a wet brush. Gently swirl it in a jar of clean water and then tap it on the rim a couple of times to remove excess water. The bristles should be fluid but not beading or dripping.

Watercolor paint is highly pigmented, and you only need a small amount to create a vibrant shade. It may be helpful to spray your set with a light mist of water before using it. The more water you add to the dab of pigment, the more diluted the color will be. Using less water will result in a more intense and vibrant color.

Try playing around with dabs of pure color and varying amounts of water on separate watercolor paper to get a feel for your chosen brush and color. I would recommend doing this with all the colors in your set, as their true shade will appear very different on paper compared to the dry pan.

BRUSHSTROKES

Round brushes are useful because you can use both the thickness and point of the brush tip to create a variety of strokes. Experiment with your collection of brushes on plain watercolor paper to see how many different thicknesses of strokes you can make. It's very handy to have at least one fine brush for small details, such as leaf veins or animal fur.

Here are some examples of brushstrokes that you can create with different brushes:

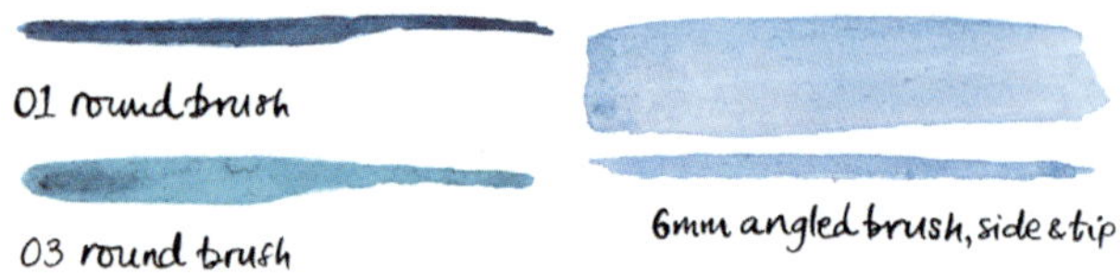

- **Wet on dry:** This simply means you're applying wet paint to a dry surface, like fresh watercolor paper or a painted page that has fully dried.
- **Wet on wet:** This is where you add wet paint to an already wet page, causing the paint to bleed with a diffused edge. This can be useful when blending, but be careful not to soak your workbook pages too much, as color may seep through the page.
- **Blending:** Two colors can be blended directly onto your piece, side by side, and then lightly merged with your damp brush. I would recommend mixing colors in your palette, however, rather than directly onto the page, so you can subtly build up the color's intensity.

LAYERING

With watercolor, it is important to start with lighter layers of color. I suggest layering from light to dark when using watercolor, but especially when working with a more vibrant color palette. Once dry, richer color and intensity can be achieved by adding more transparent layers, a technique that is often called "glazing." The more layers, the darker and more intense the color will be.

- **Initial layer:** You may think after an initial light wash of color that your page looks a bit boring and lacks vibrancy, but have patience and let the page dry before adding more color (some people keep a hair dryer on hand for this very purpose!). Think about this almost as the "white" areas of the design, which will be visible after adding further layers. If you'd like some true white to peep through at the end, add masking fluid to those areas before beginning.

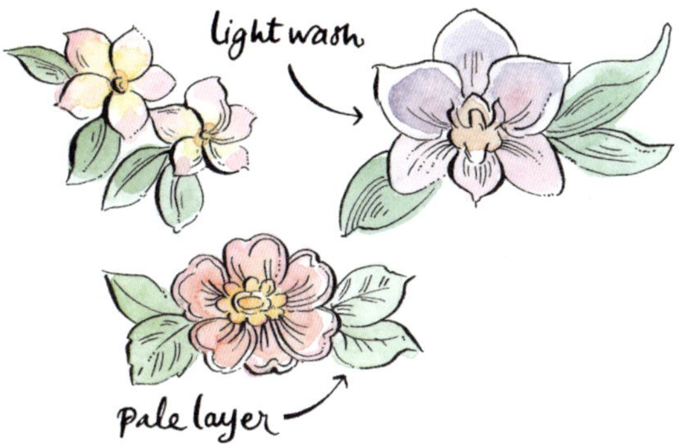

- **Second and subsequent layers:** Here is where you can build up the intensity of the color. Think about which parts of the design might be in the fore- or background. Add more layers of color under images to create shadows and depth. The same rules apply with bright rather than muted colors: layering is essential. If you'd like to create more patterned designs, use a second or third layer to add contrasting color or texture with a fine brush.

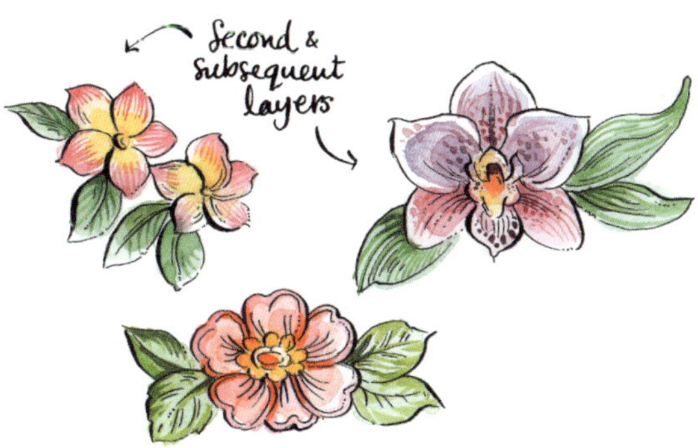

- **Layering with bright color:** The temptation is to mix a bright fresh palette and dive in and cover the whole page with vibrant color! However, exercise caution; with watercolor, it's easy to build color intensity gradually but nearly impossible to remove strong pigment. Layering can create vibrancy without over-saturating your page with strong color.

LAYERING EXERCISE WITH BRIGHT GREEN

On a clean sheet of watercolor/cartridge paper, draw out this simple grid below with a faint pencil line.

Mix your green shade, aiming for a bright and vibrant leaf-green color (a cool blue or yellow will also work well).

With a clean pot of water and corner of your palette, add a couple of clean swirls of water, then carefully dot a small amount of your mixed color to create a transparent pale green shade. Paint your initial layer by covering the whole grid, then leave to dry.

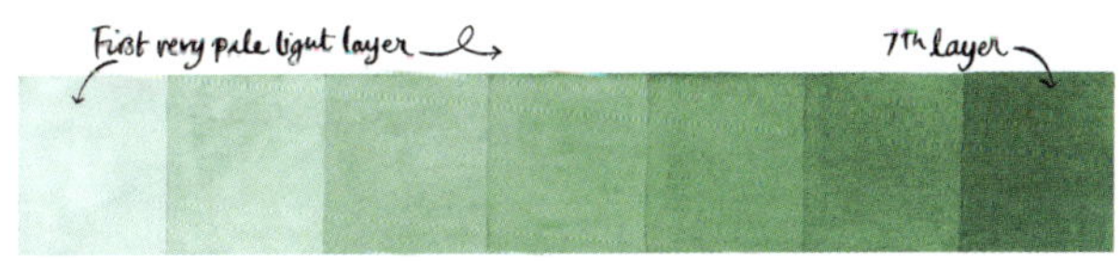

Incrementally add more and more dabs of paint to the palette, and paint successive layers of transparent color, starting one square to the right from where you started the last layer, to build the intensity and tone.

Color

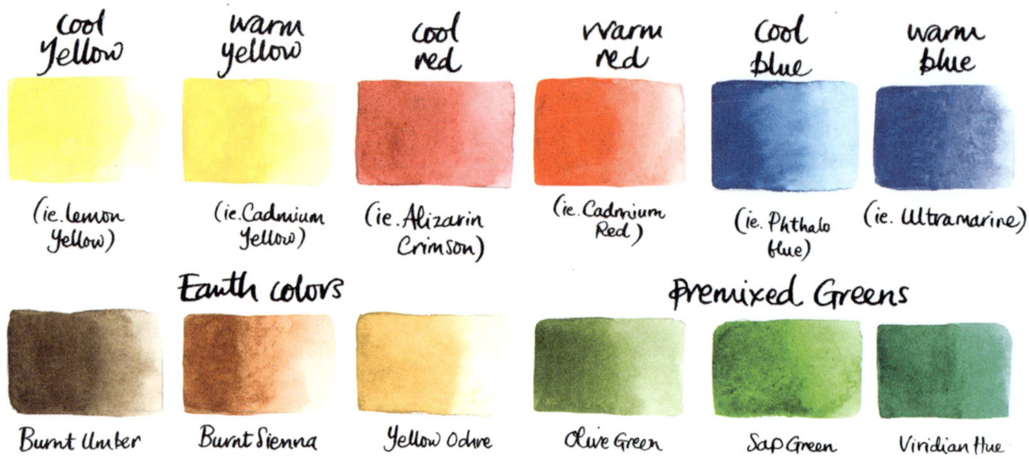

Understanding the basics of color theory is useful when considering how to choose and paint your designs. You will be able to mix a vibrant range of colors with even a small watercolor set. Most sets will contain two of each of the primary colors: red, yellow, and blue—one will be "warm" and one "cool." There will also be some useful earth tones such as burnt sienna, burnt umber, and yellow ochre, and often a white that you can use to create pastel shades.

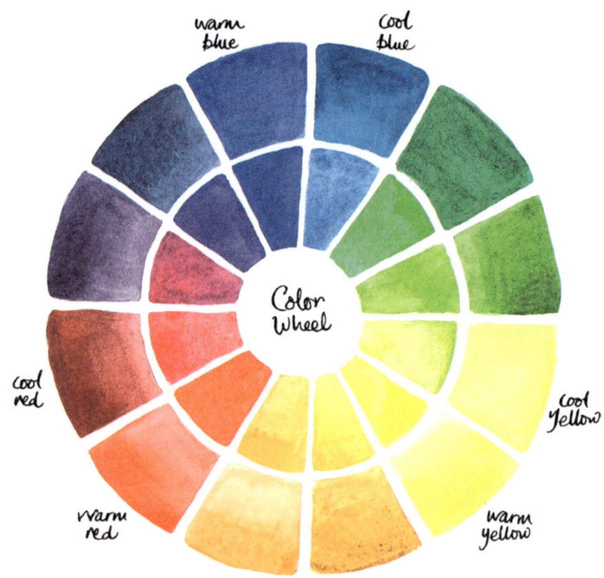

COLOR MIXING

This color wheel gives a simple visual explanation of how to mix an array of colors.

Complementary colors sit opposite each other on the wheel, such as pink and green and blue and orange. They may appear jarring at first glance, but used subtly, they can create wonderfully surprising combinations.

BLACK

Black must be used very sparingly to avoid creating a lifeless, dull color. Most sets will not include black, but you can easily mix your own soft dark shade. You can do this in countless variations, but generally speaking, adding all three primary colors together creates a very dark paint.

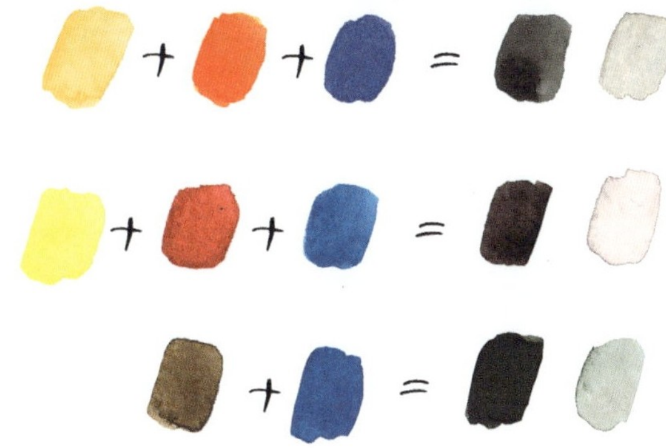

WHITE: MASKING FLUID AND WHITE GOUACHE

Your use of white is something to be considered before you begin painting. With watercolor, the only way to maintain a light area in your work is by keeping your chosen area free of paint—in other words, using the white of the page as your "white."

One way to maintain the brightness of the paper is to use masking fluid, which is also called "drawing gum." This is a liquid latex–based solution, which, when dried, resists watercolor pigment. To use it, paint it onto areas you would like to keep white (masking fluid is often tinted blue so you can see what you are doing). Then continue working on your piece as normal. When the paint is dry, simply rub off the masking fluid with an eraser or your finger, and the original white of the page will be revealed.

You can apply masking fluid with an old brush or other tools, such as a clean dip or ruling pen. Masking fluid dries almost immediately, so be sure to have a clean jar of water to wash your brush immediately, or the bristles will stick together, rendering it useless!

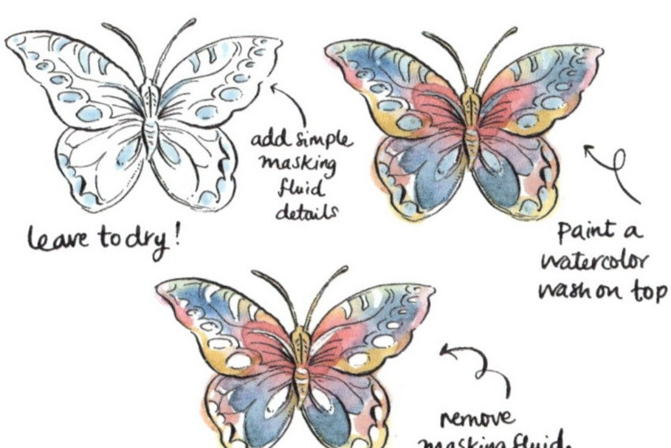

It is also very effective to add masking fluid to an already painted area, then adding further painted layers to create depth.

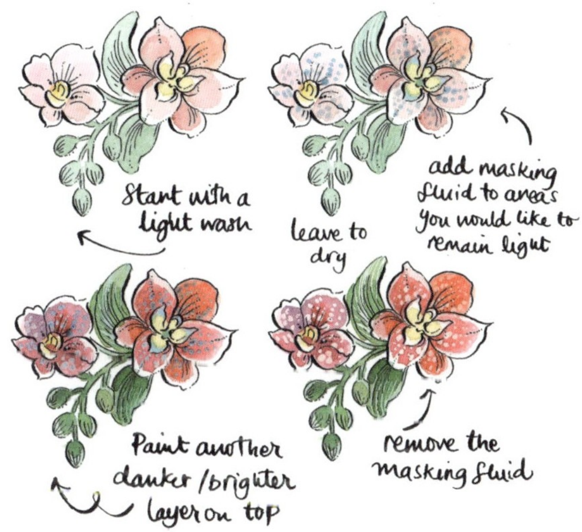

You can go even further by adding darker/brighter layers once the masking fluid is removed!

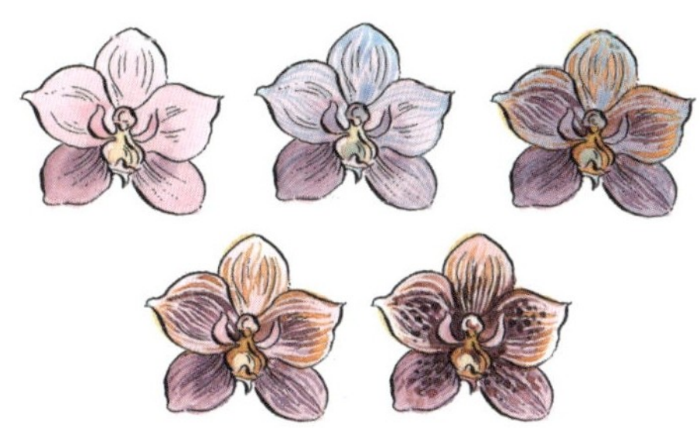

You can also use white gouache paint to add light highlights. Gouache is an opaque, water-based paint that comes in tubes rather than pans. A small blob can be thinned with water to the consistency of watercolor and even mixed with watercolor paints to create semi-opaque pastel shades.

To keep areas of white fresh and bright, I would recommend using masking fluid first and keeping gouache in your emergency reserve!

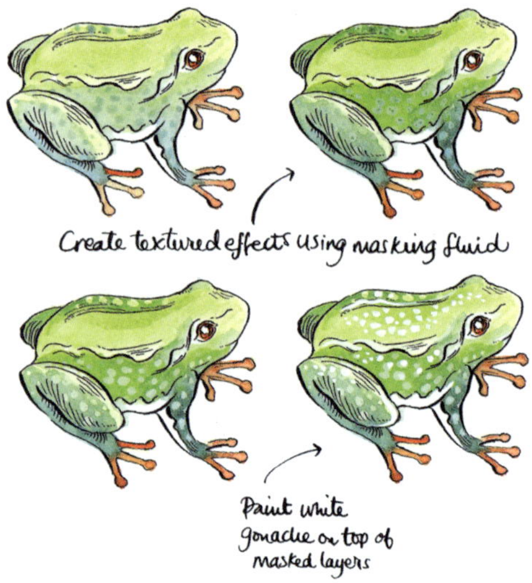

MIXING AND USING GREEN

Rainforests are abundant with vibrant and luscious green shades, which will be needed for the designs in this book. Below are some examples of premixed greens that can easily be adjusted or desaturated with the addition of browns, greys, blues, and yellows.

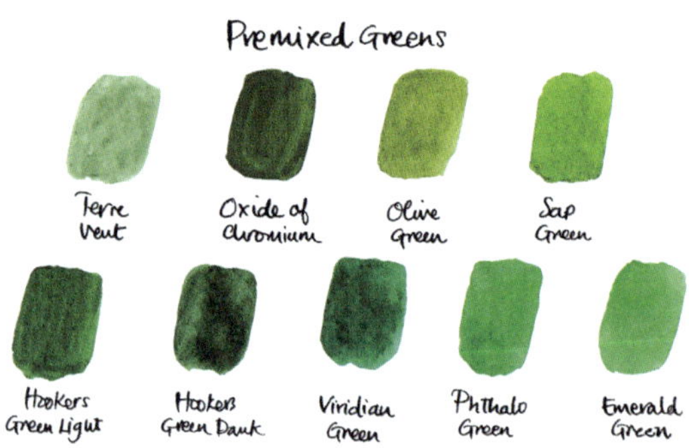

Some premixed colors in sets and tubes can look very unnatural, so here is a quick guide to mixing your own realistic shades. Mixing the primary colors of blue and yellow will create green.

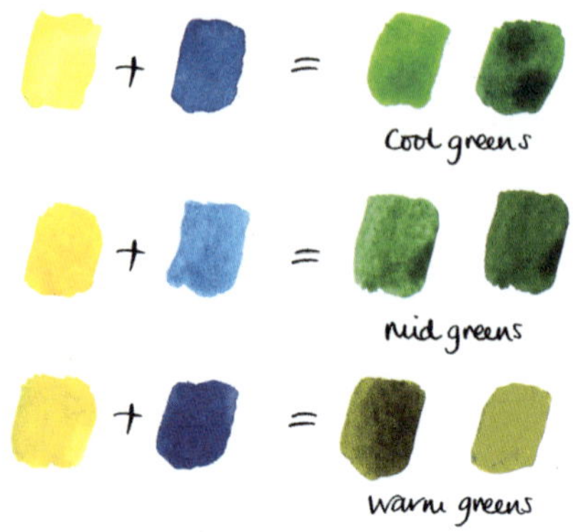

Cool greens are created by mixing cool yellows (i.e. Lemon Yellow) and blues (i.e. Phthalo Blue) together, as they lean more towards blue and combined create a bright fresh range of greens.

Mid greens can often be mixed from premixed neutral blues (i.e. Cobalt Blue) and yellows (i.e. Mid Yellow). I will often adjust by adding more yellow, blue, or brown.

Warm greens are created by mixing warm yellows (i.e. Cadmium Yellow) and blues (i.e. Ultramarine) together, as they lean more towards red and combined create a more muted earthy palette.

Muted or earthy greens can be created by adding an earthy tone such as Burnt Sienna, Burnt Umber, or Payne's Grey to any of your mixed primary greens to create an array of muted, earthy greens.

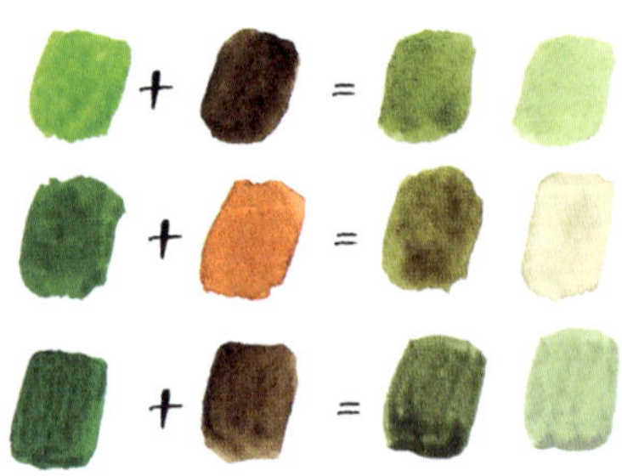

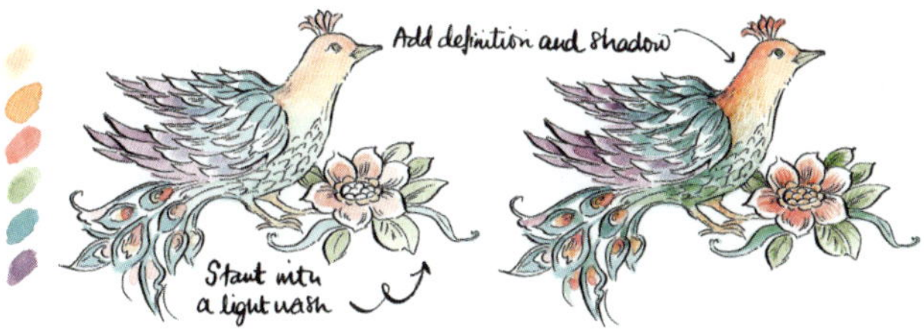

IMAGINATIVE COLOR

Lots of the birds and flower illustrations in this book are suggestively imaginative. Let's embrace this! Think about premixing a non-realistic palette of colors (checking with swatches that they work well together) and then use this on a page. You'll be surprised where your imagination will take you!

USING ONE OR TWO COLORS

This is a very simple and enjoyable way of working on a design and can be relatively quick, as you need minimal color mixing. It's perfect for the days when you need some relaxing downtime.

Single color: Choose one shade that you like and mix enough in your palette to work on the whole page. Working in light layers, build up the color either to replicate shadow or to fill in areas of negative space. Think of the white of the page as the contrasting color, so leave some areas unpainted.

TIP: Blue and white is a classic pairing!

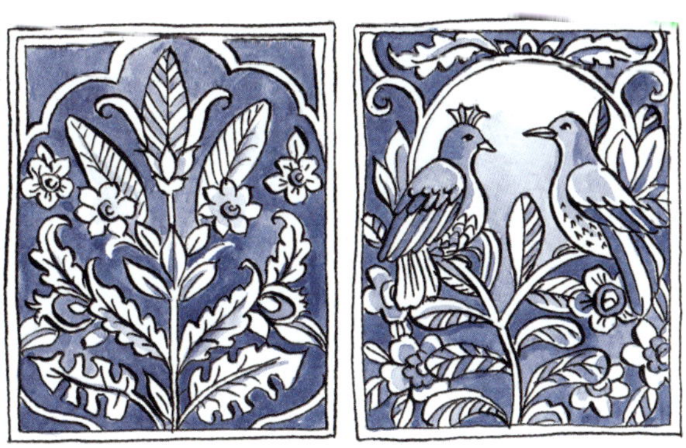

Two colors: Use the same premise as with one color, and think of the white of the page almost as the third color. Choose two colors that complement each other on the color wheel, such as pink and green. See below for a few of my favorite combinations that you could try.

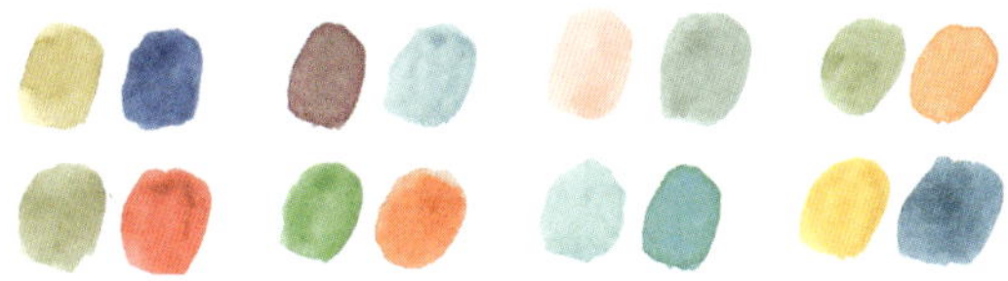

CHOOSING YOUR COLORS

You've opened your workbook, chosen your favorite designs, and have your paint set and brushes ready, now what? Where should you start and how do you create an inspired color palette?

TRY RESEARCH

Try searching for images online to see photos of real rainforest flora and fauna. What colors do we see in tropical butterflies, flowers, or rainforest leaves? Do you live near a botanical garden you might be able to visit and paint or draw in?

Enjoy browsing books or online museum galleries to see how both artists of the past and present might paint a rainforest. Some artists to look up might be Henri Rousseau or Marianne North. I find the use of color and pattern by contemporary print designers very inspiring, as well as textile and home furnishing patterns and wallpaper companies.

NATURE INSPIRATION

Nature boasts such a wonderful range of colors that we can draw inspiration from. Try asking yourself a few questions about the drawing to help you come to some decisions about your palette. What time of day do you imagine it to be and what direction is the light coming from? Will the scene contain rich bright hues on a sunny day or have a dark sky and only a few pops of color?

Techniques for Using Your Workbook

Here are a few techniques that may be helpful to consider as you use your workbook.

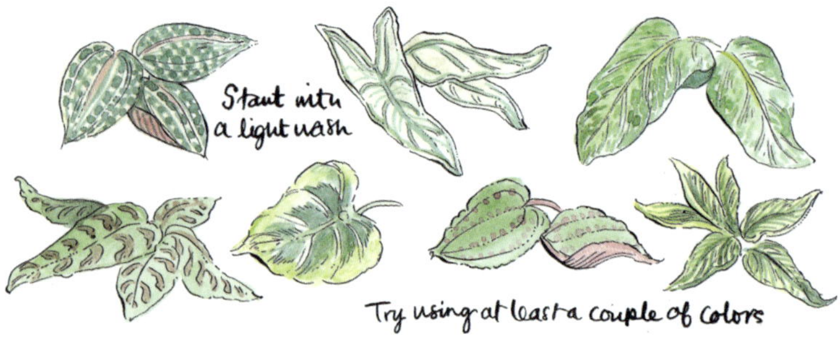

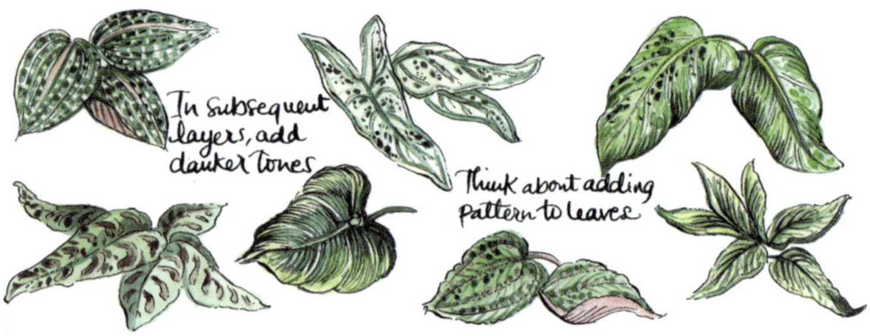

PAINTING LEAVES & FOLIAGE

Now that you've practiced mixing your greens, it's time to apply them to the leaves and undergrowth of the forest! Layer carefully, leaving areas of light and building depth layer by layer.

Try blending different shades on one leaf and embrace the imperfections that you'd find in real leaves. Also think about the kind of patterns you might find on a tropical leaf: this is where you can really go to town!

Adding areas of shadow to leaves and foliage creates depth in the designs, particularly with full rainforest scenes.

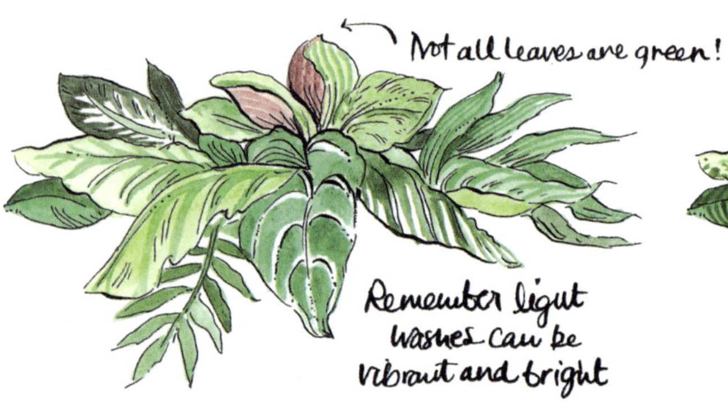

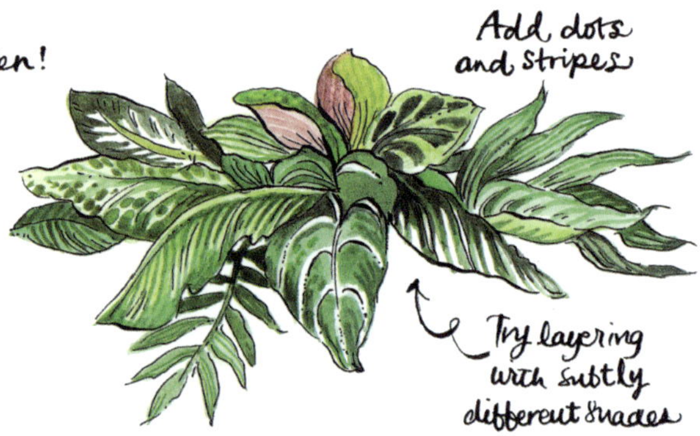

PAINTING FUR

There is an abundance of furry creatures to be found in the rainforest. Create texture by building soft layers of color with detailed strokes using a fine brush.

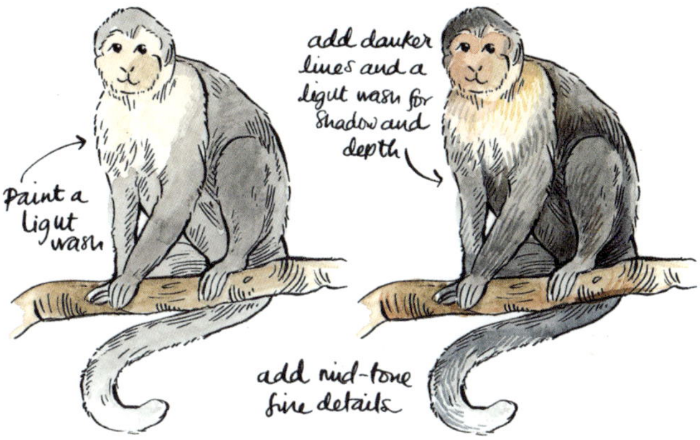

PAINTING FEATHERS

Begin with light, translucent layers of blocked-out color. Next, add fine, curved, soft strokes to suggest feathered details.

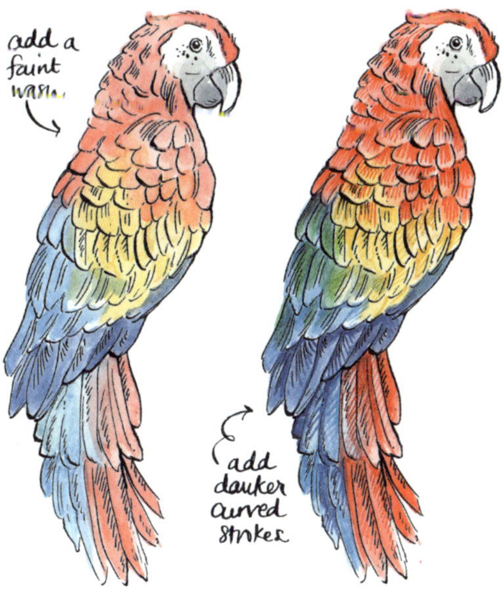

WATERCOLOR PENCILS

These are a very useful addition to your kit, although not strictly necessary. Watercolor pencils really complement watercolor paint, and they have the bonus of being easier to control, especially with fine details. Watercolor pencils can be used in a couple of ways:

A. Color your page with the pencil and then use a wash of water to blend and create a paint-like effect.

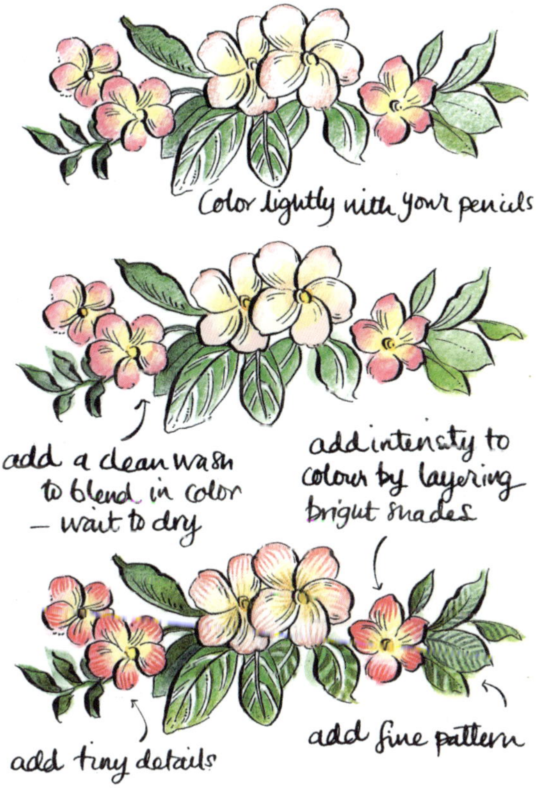

B. Use watercolor pencils to add details to your watercolor paintings. This can be done in a couple of ways: wet or dry. If you draw with watercolor pencils directly onto a damp or wet page, the pigment can be very bright and rich but also difficult to remove. If you draw on dry paper, you can create a variety of layers and intensity of color by adding a little water wash.

TIP: Bear in mind that your paper will be weaker when wet and drawing on top may add texture to the surface of the paper or even create holes!

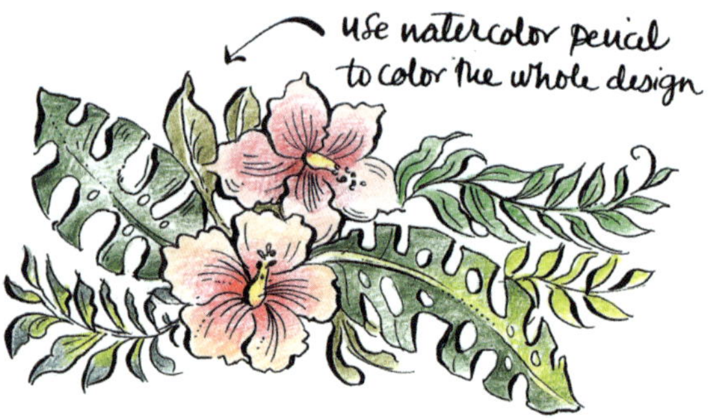

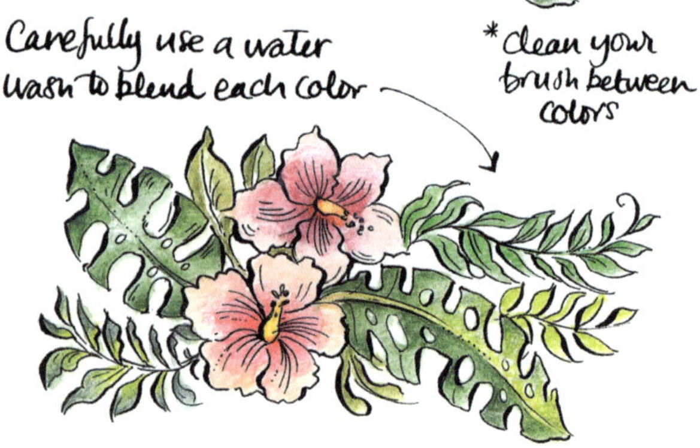

ADDING DETAILS OUTSIDE THE LINES

One of the joys of working with ink and wash drawings is the opportunity to splash about—you don't have to only paint inside lines. Use the example below to inspire your work.

Experimentation is always the best place to start with your workbook, and daunting though a fresh page might be, it's your personal space and the more you work through the book, the more your confidence will grow!

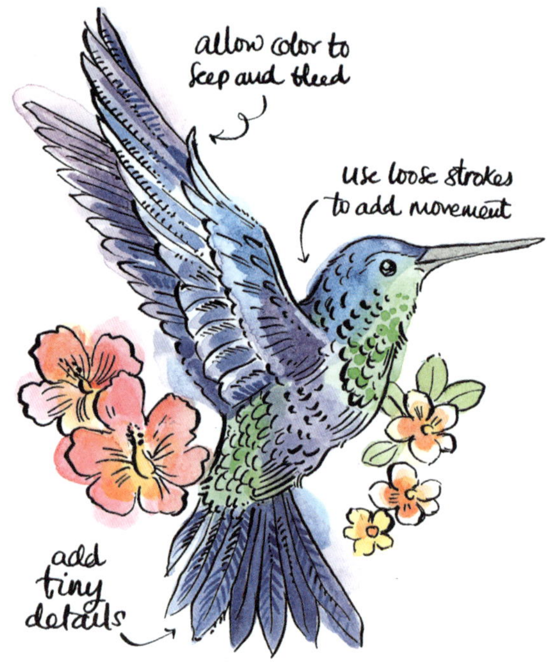

Getting Started With Your Workbook

TIPS

- Flatten your page down from the central binding before starting work so that you have a nice flat surface to work with. Clip the pages flat, if necessary.
- Try keeping a spare page of watercolor or cartridge paper on hand to check the vibrancy and consistency of your color before painting in the workbook.
- Choose your second or third favorite page to start; you'll be excited to work with the design, but some of the pressure of "ruining" your favorite will be alleviated!
- You can easily remove watercolor paint when it's still wet by lightly dabbing it with clean water and then removing this with clean paper towels. Always leave it to dry before working on top so that you don't damage the surface of the paper.

DON'T FORGET

- Prop open any wet pages so that they do not stick together when drying.
- Although this is medium-grade watercolor paper, be careful not to add too much water when painting a page. Have tissues or paper towels on hand to blot if necessary!
- Overworking wet pages can damage the paper—leaving each layer to dry will help with this.

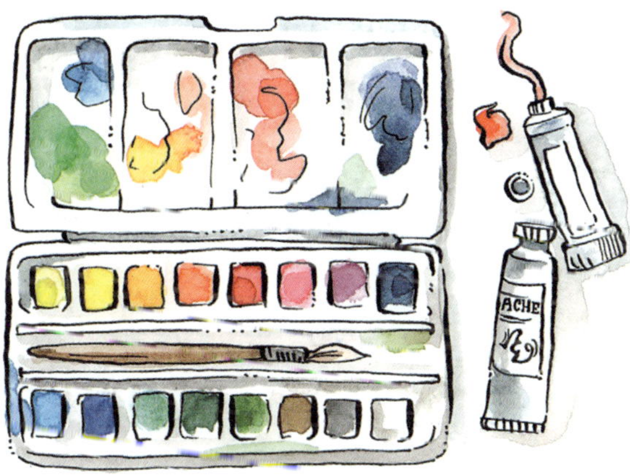

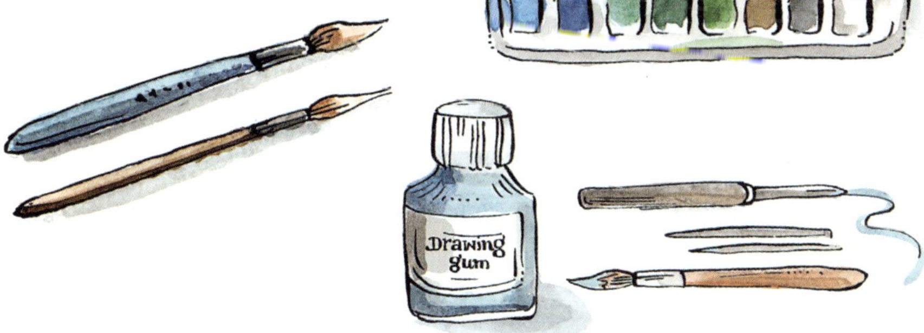

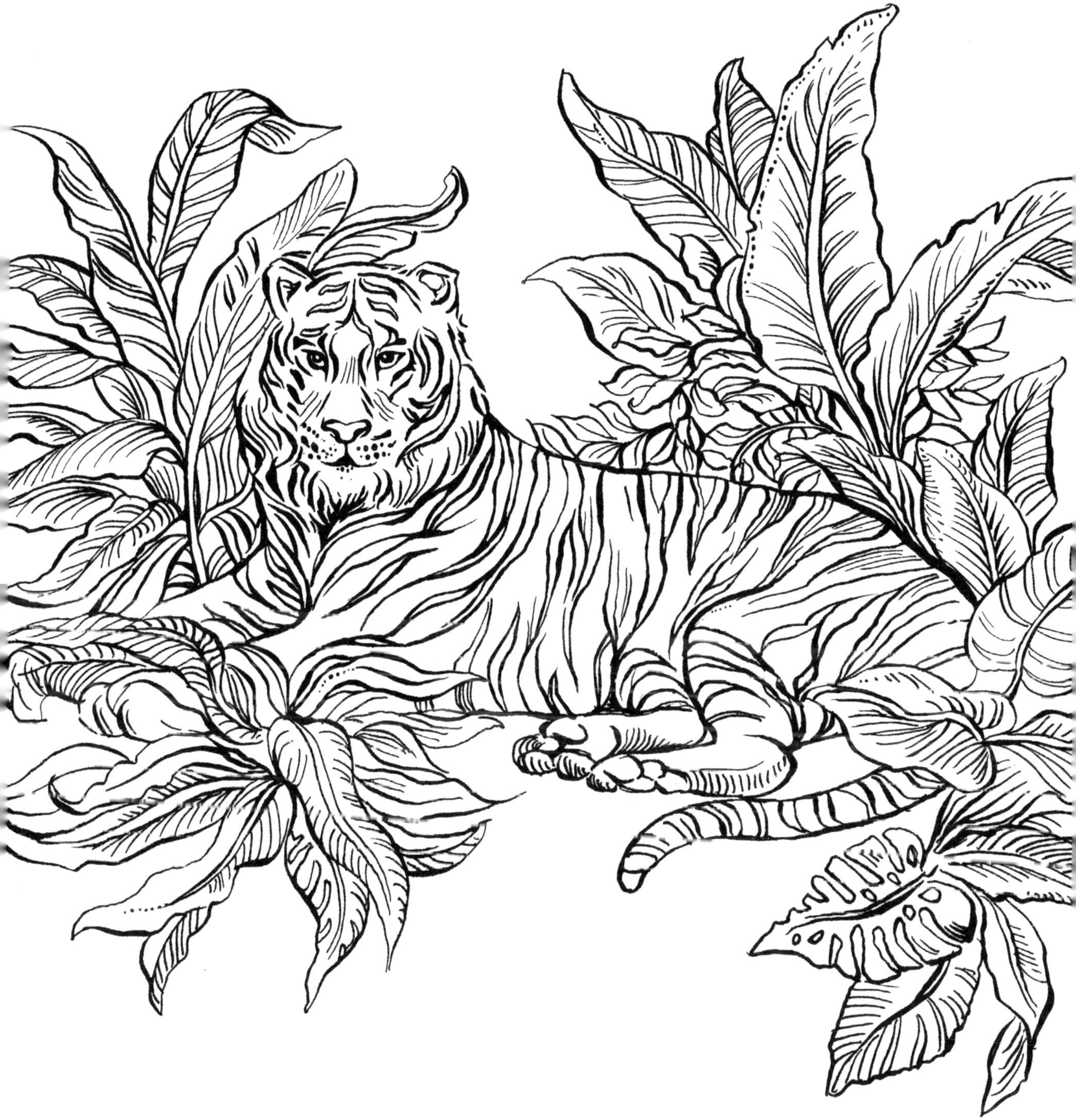

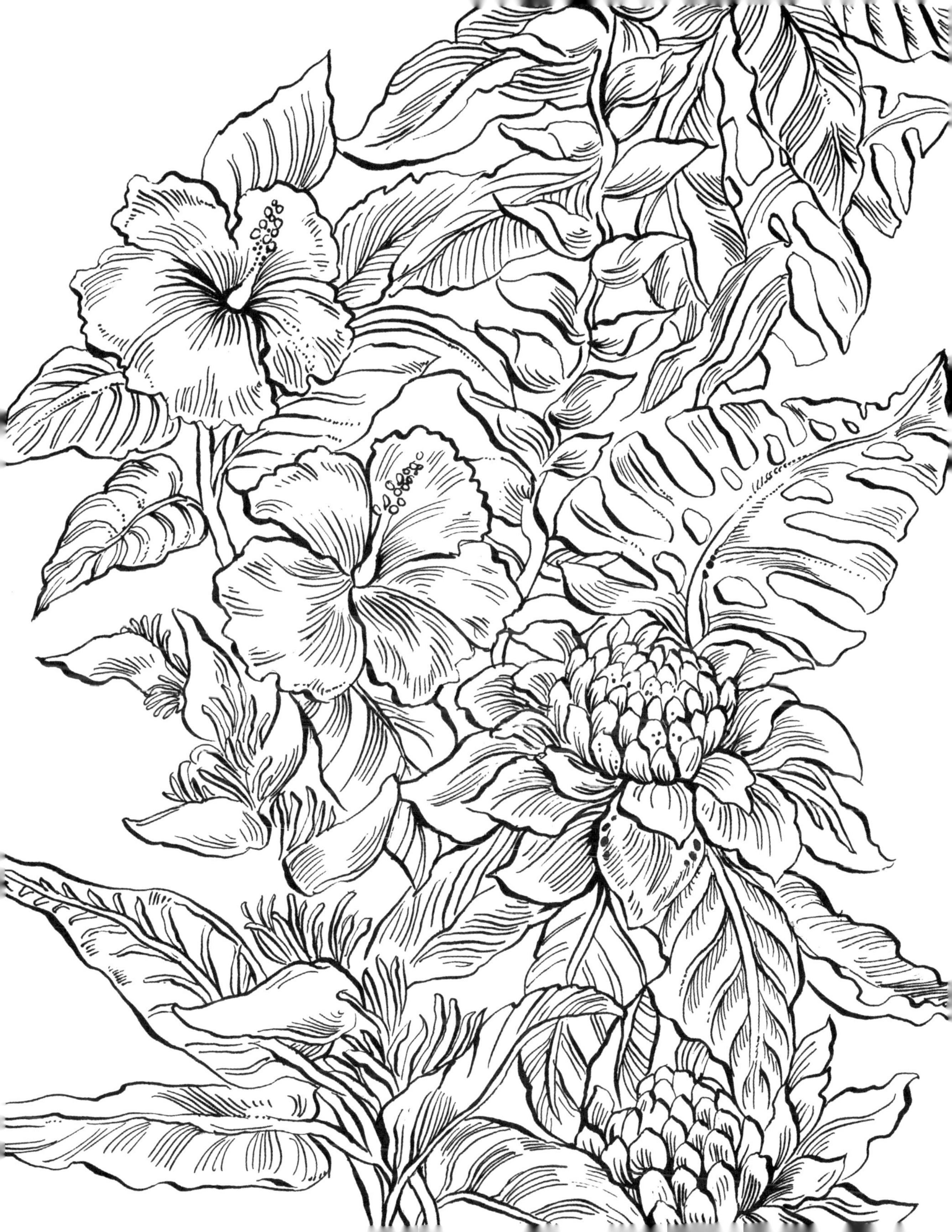

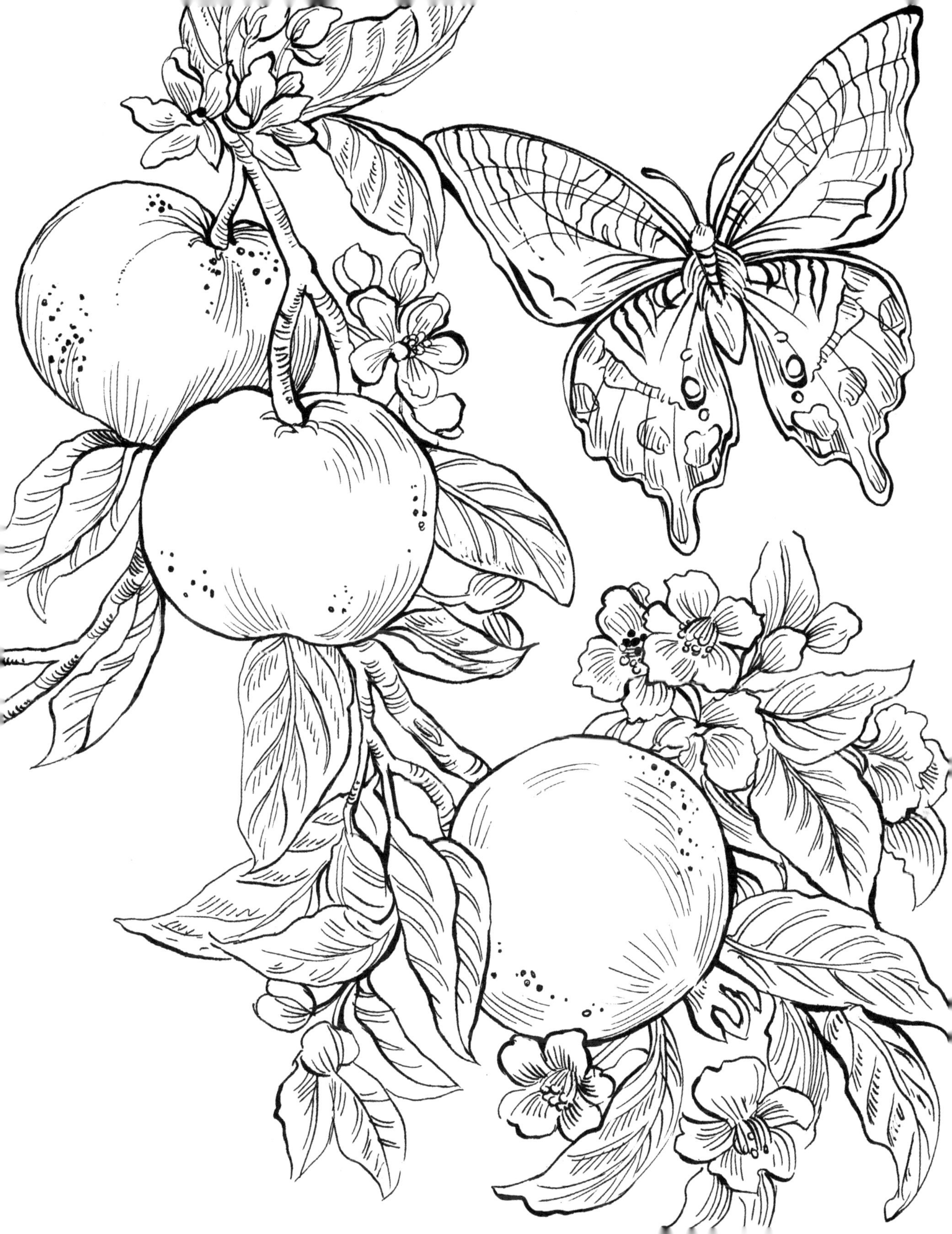

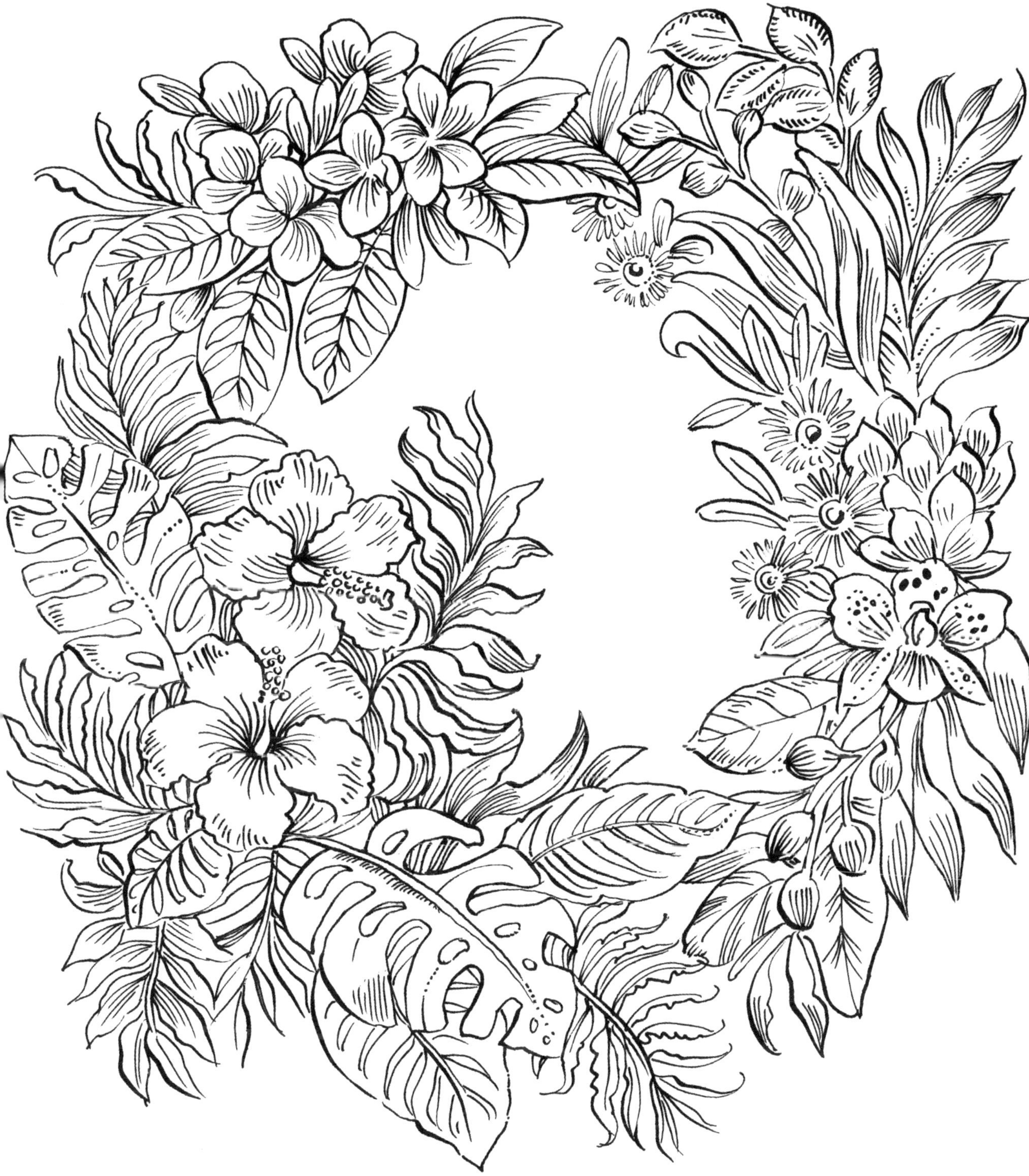

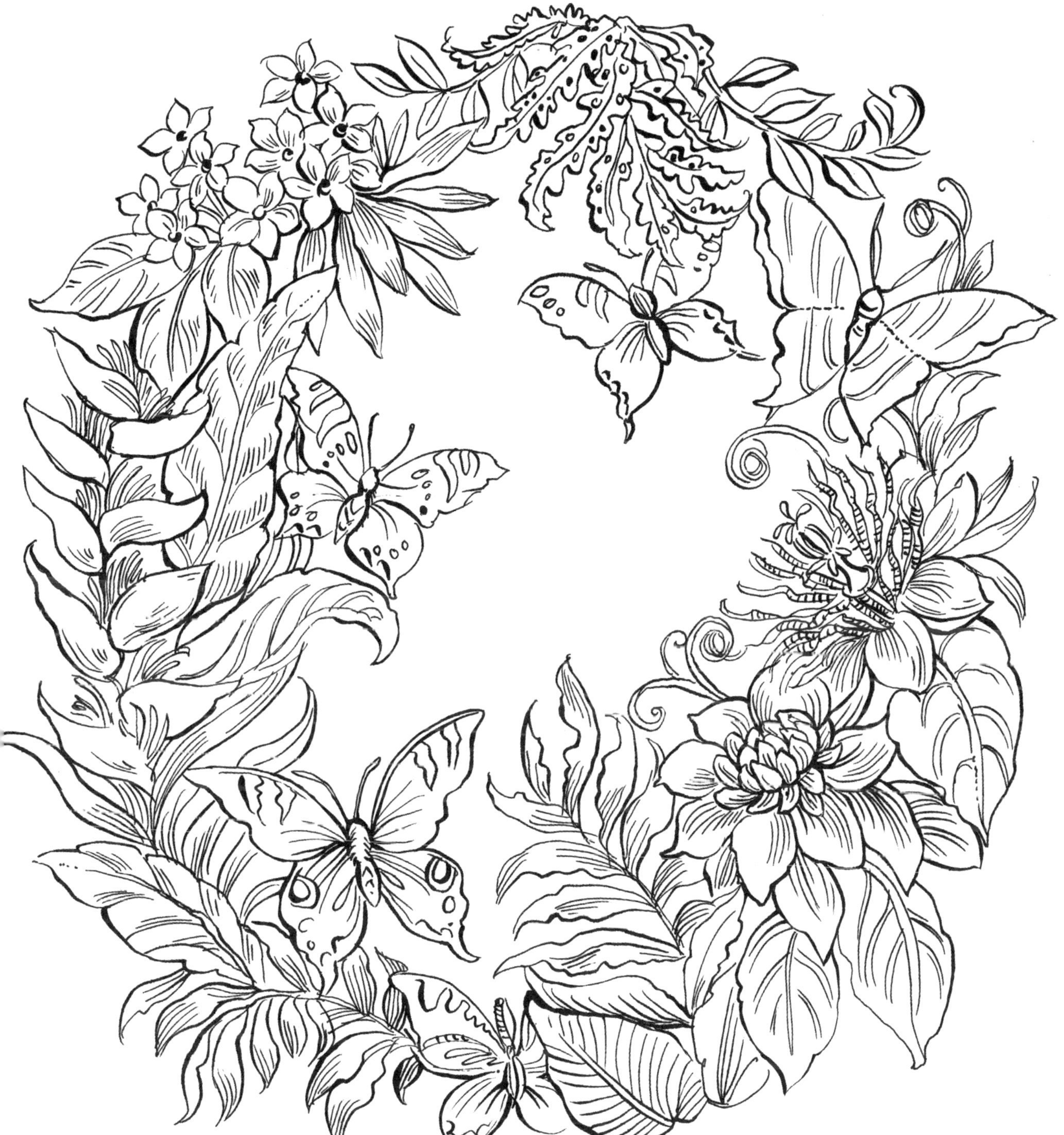

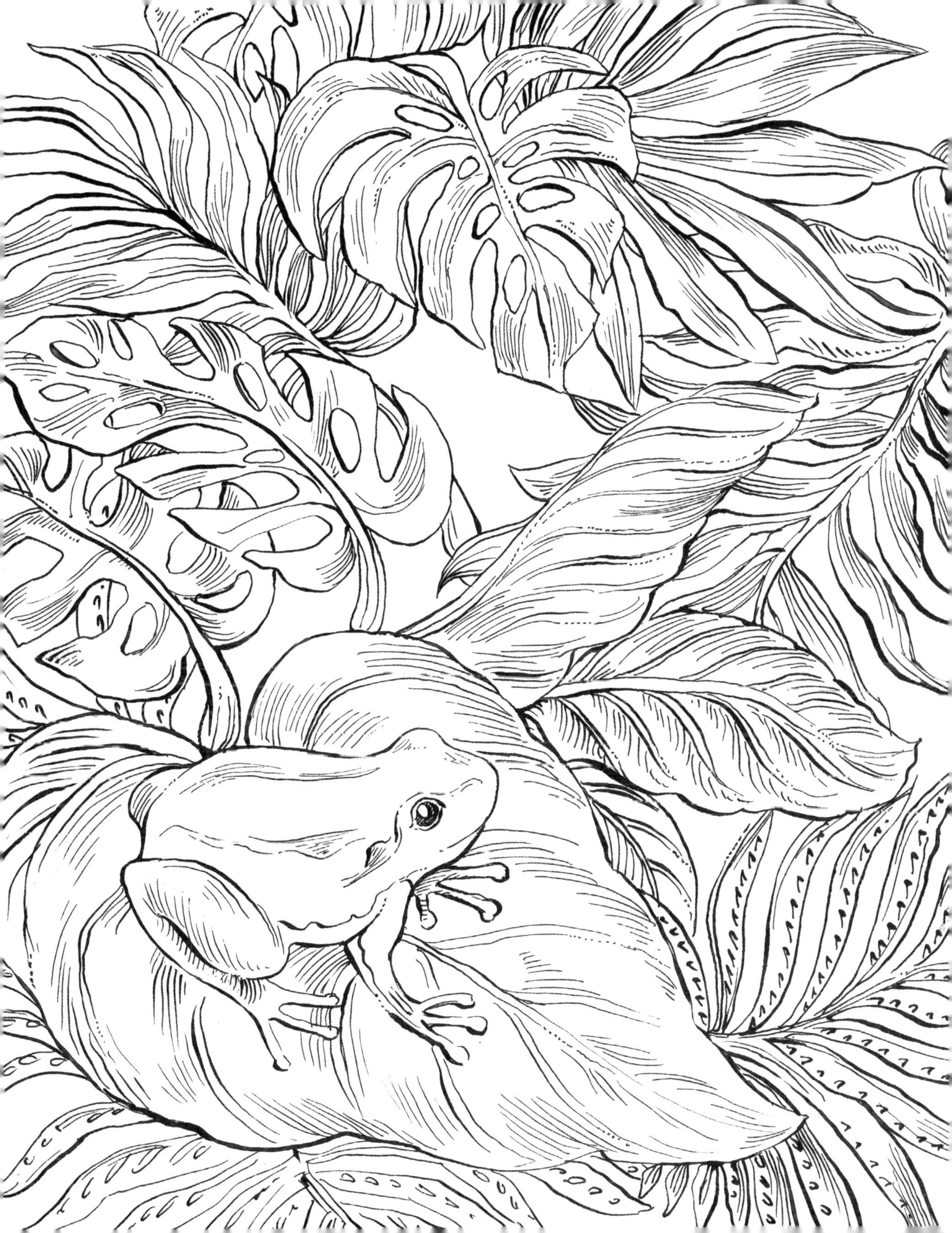

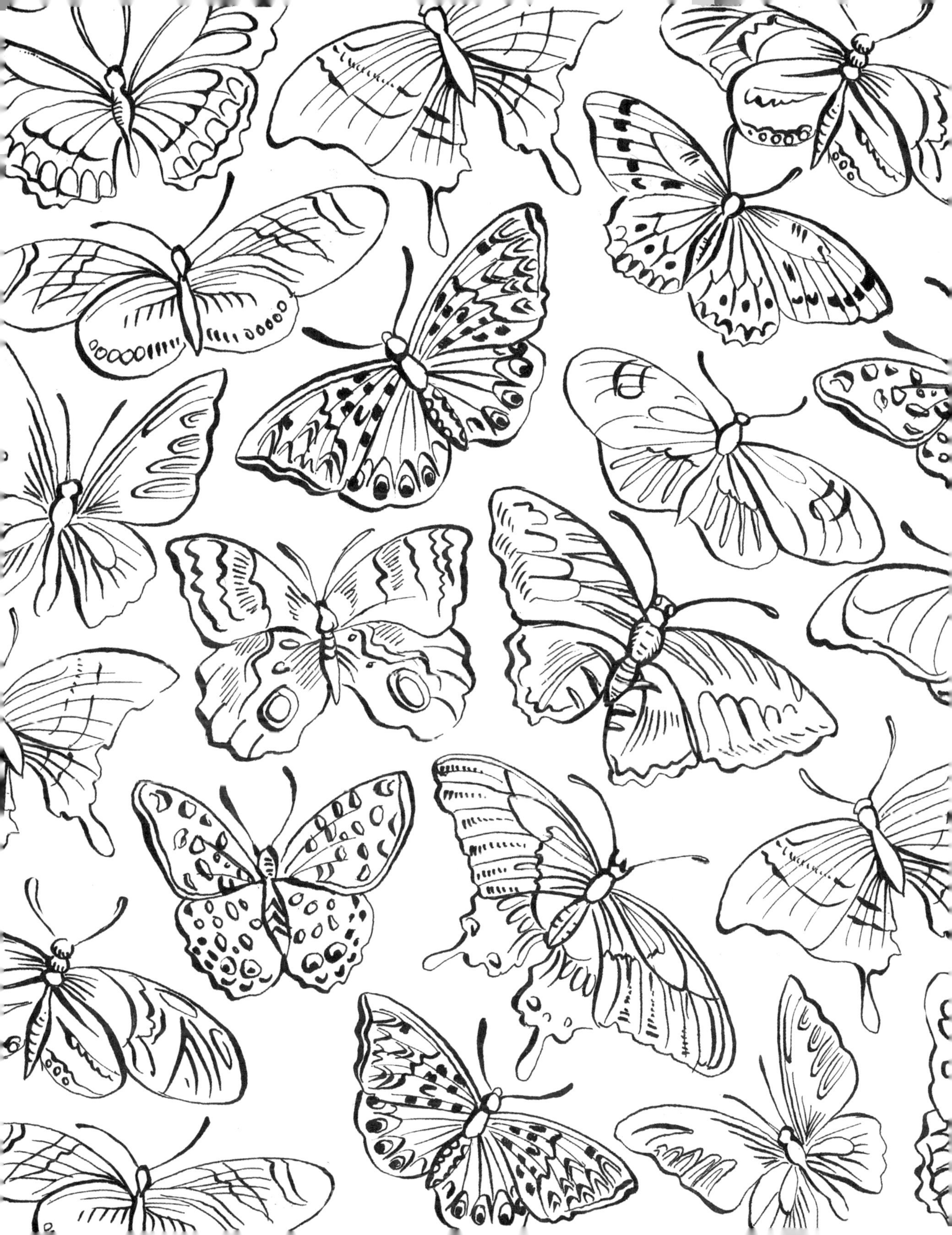

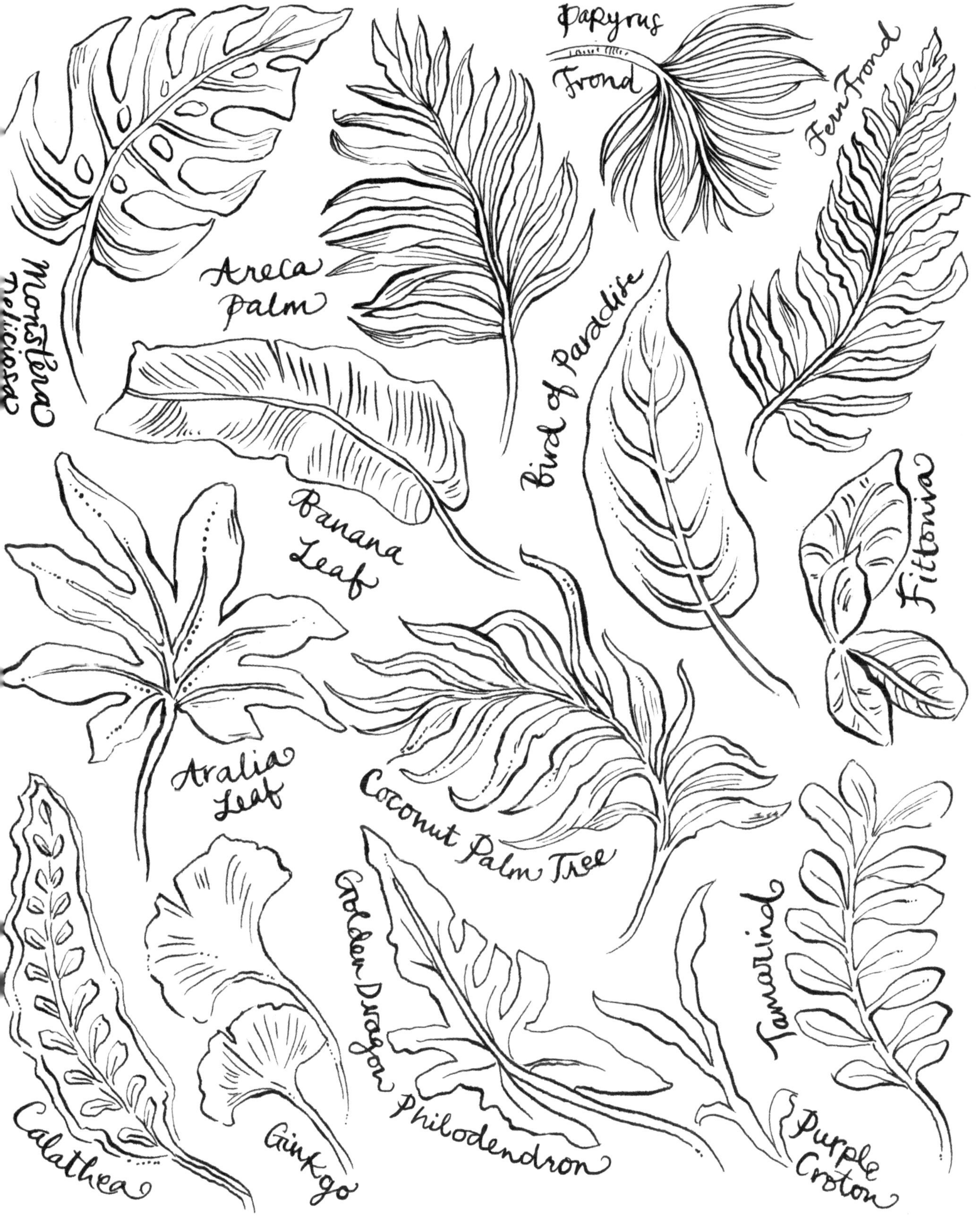
Papyrus
Frond
Fern Frond
Monstera Deliciosa
Areca Palm
Bird of Paradise
Banana Leaf
Fittonia
Aralia Leaf
Coconut Palm Tree
Golden Dragon
Tamarind
Calathea
Ginkgo
Philodendron
Purple Croton

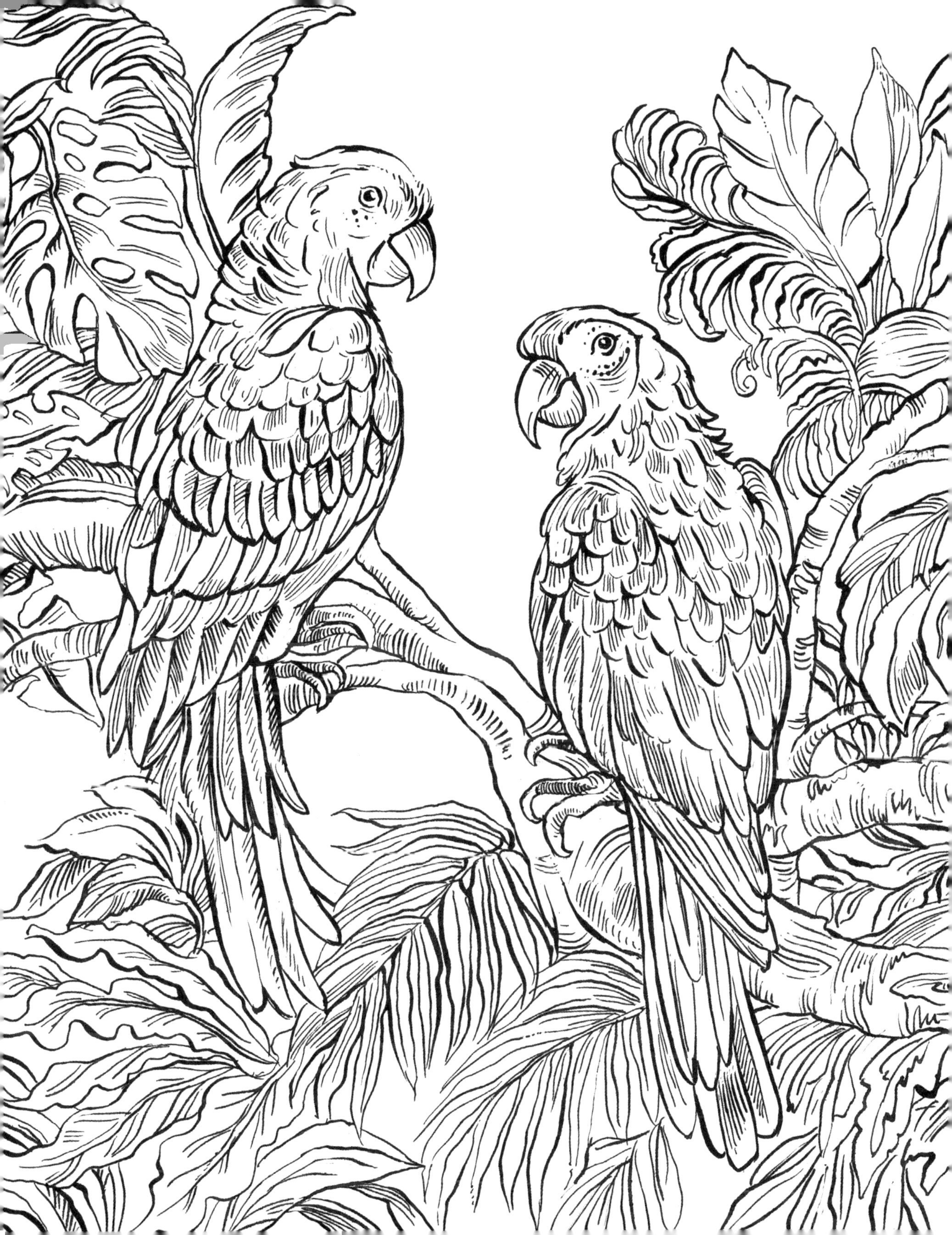

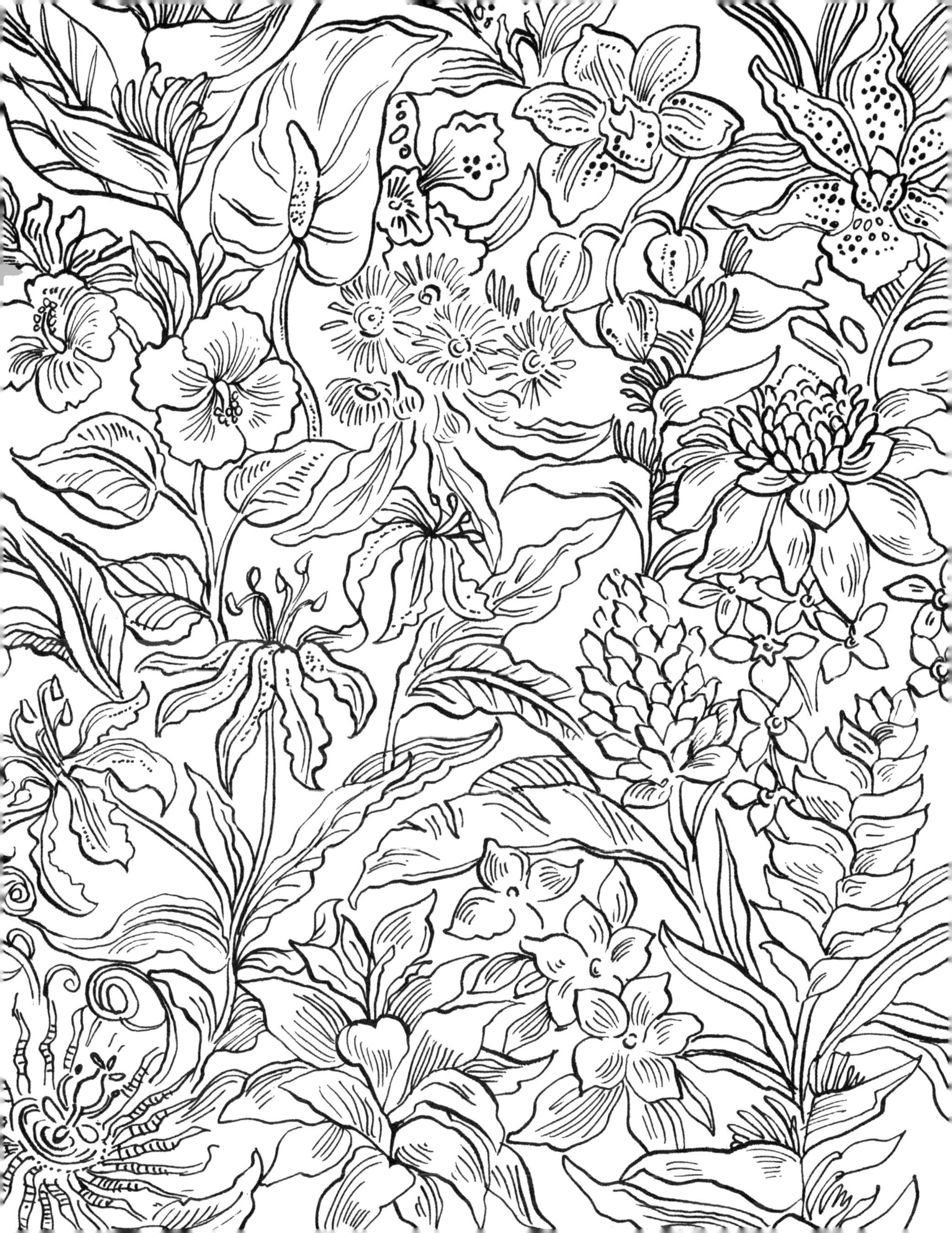

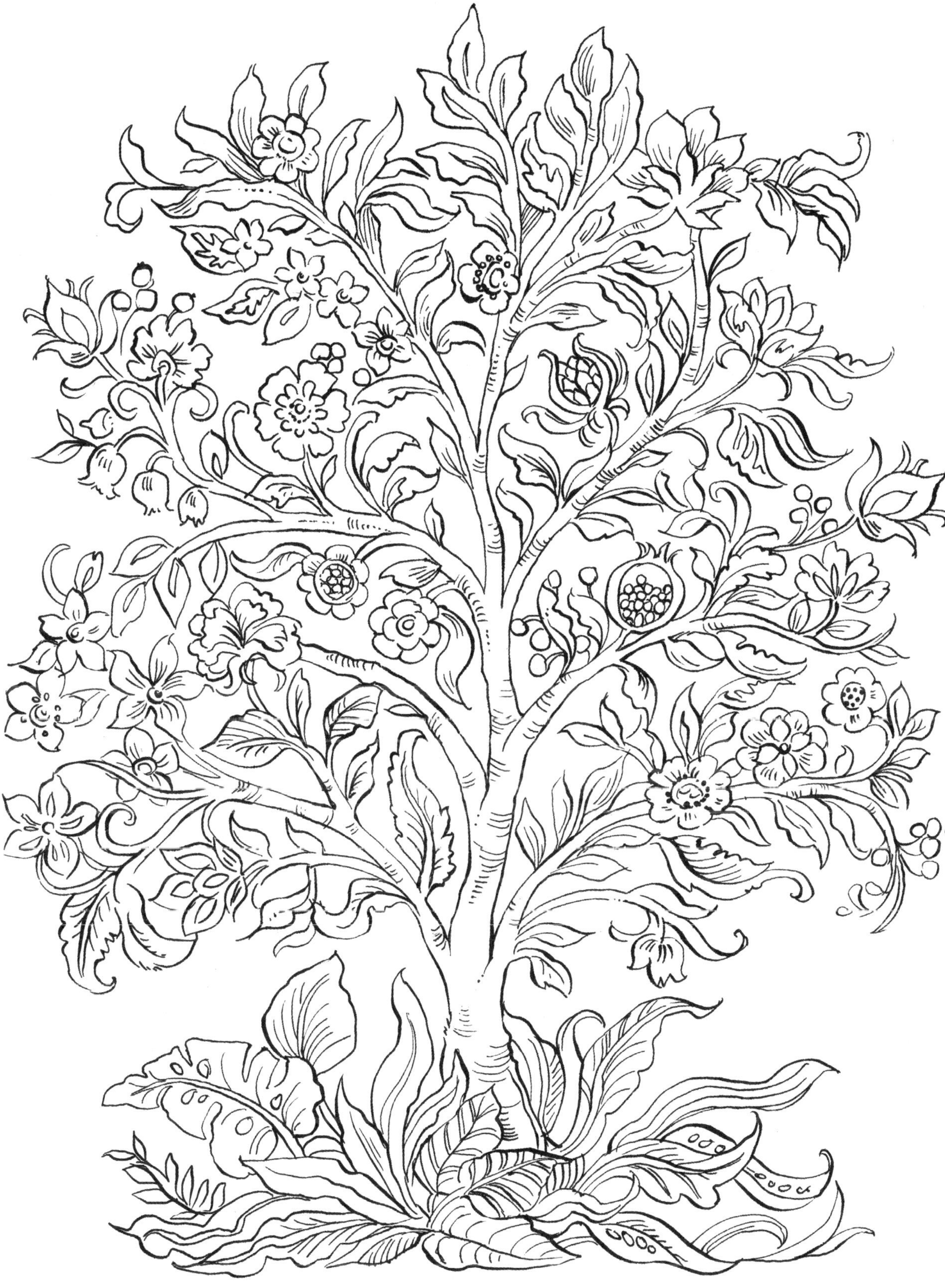

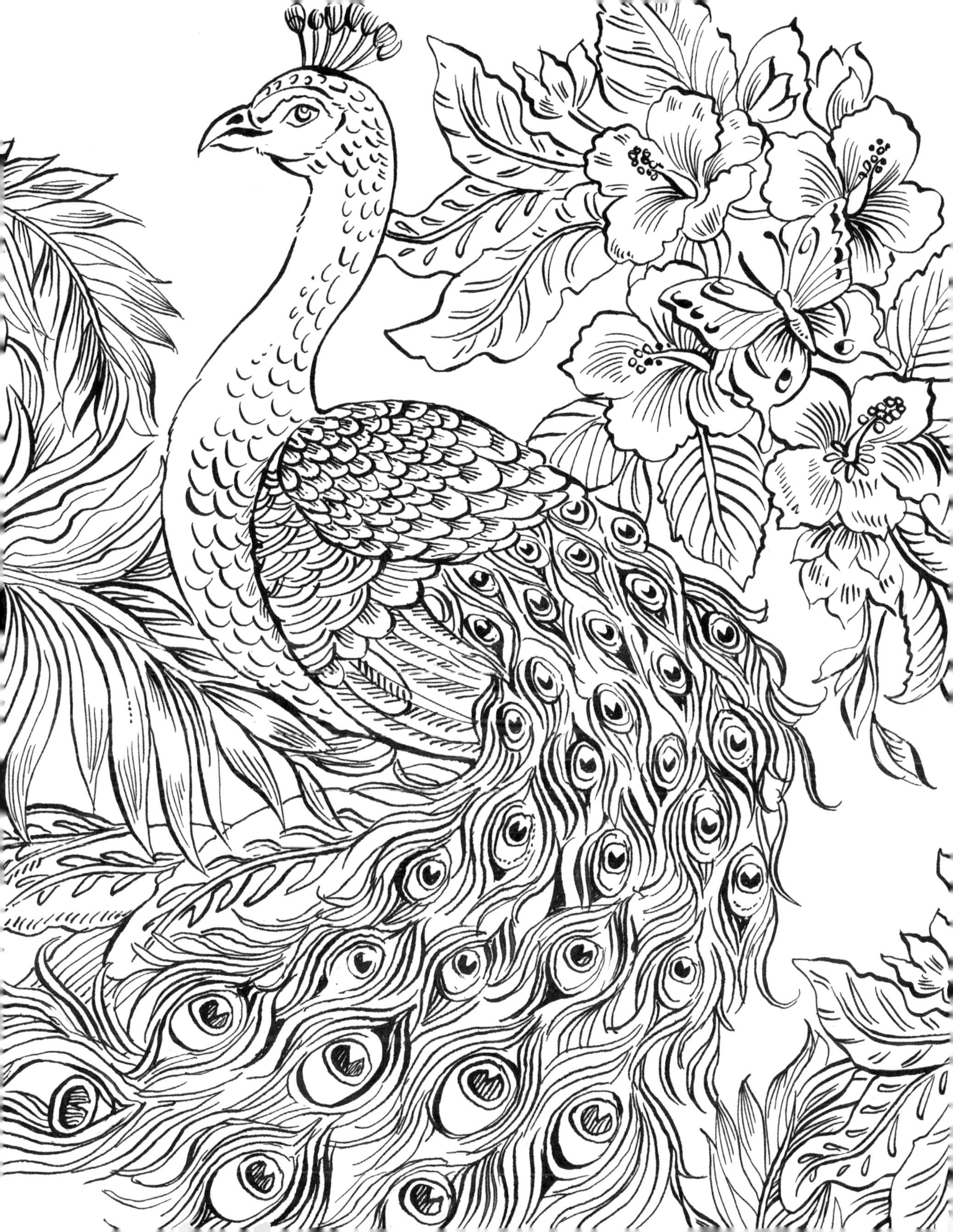

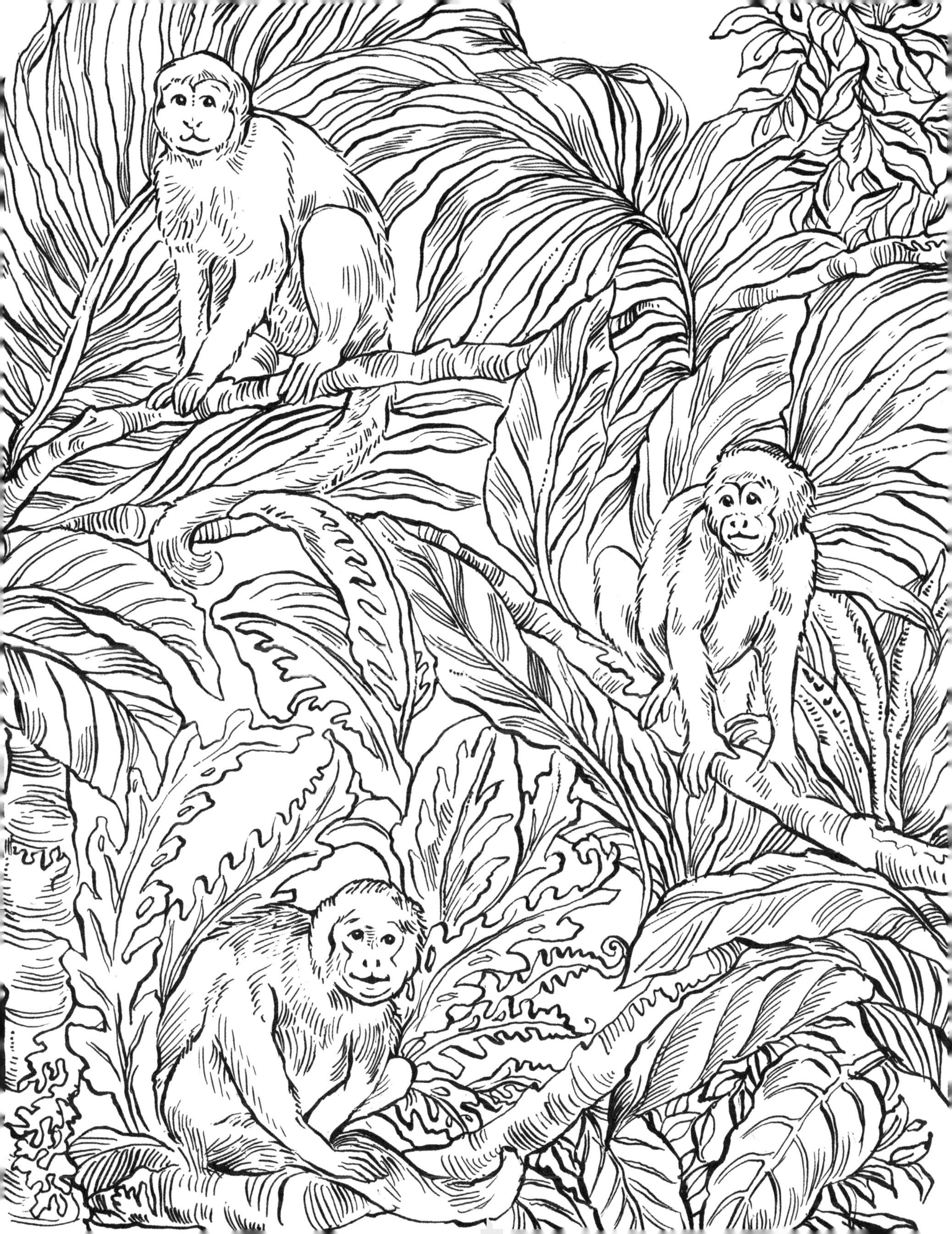

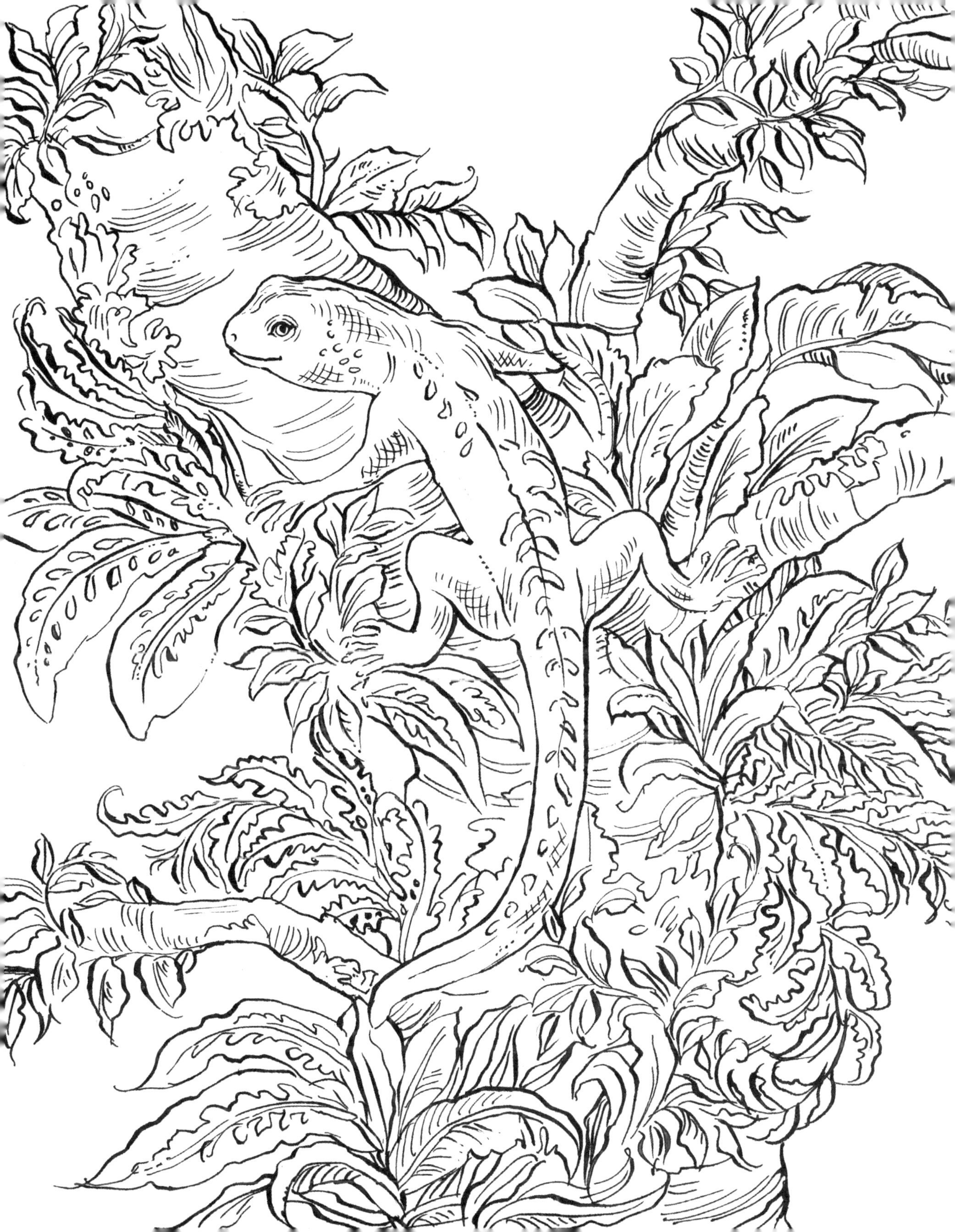

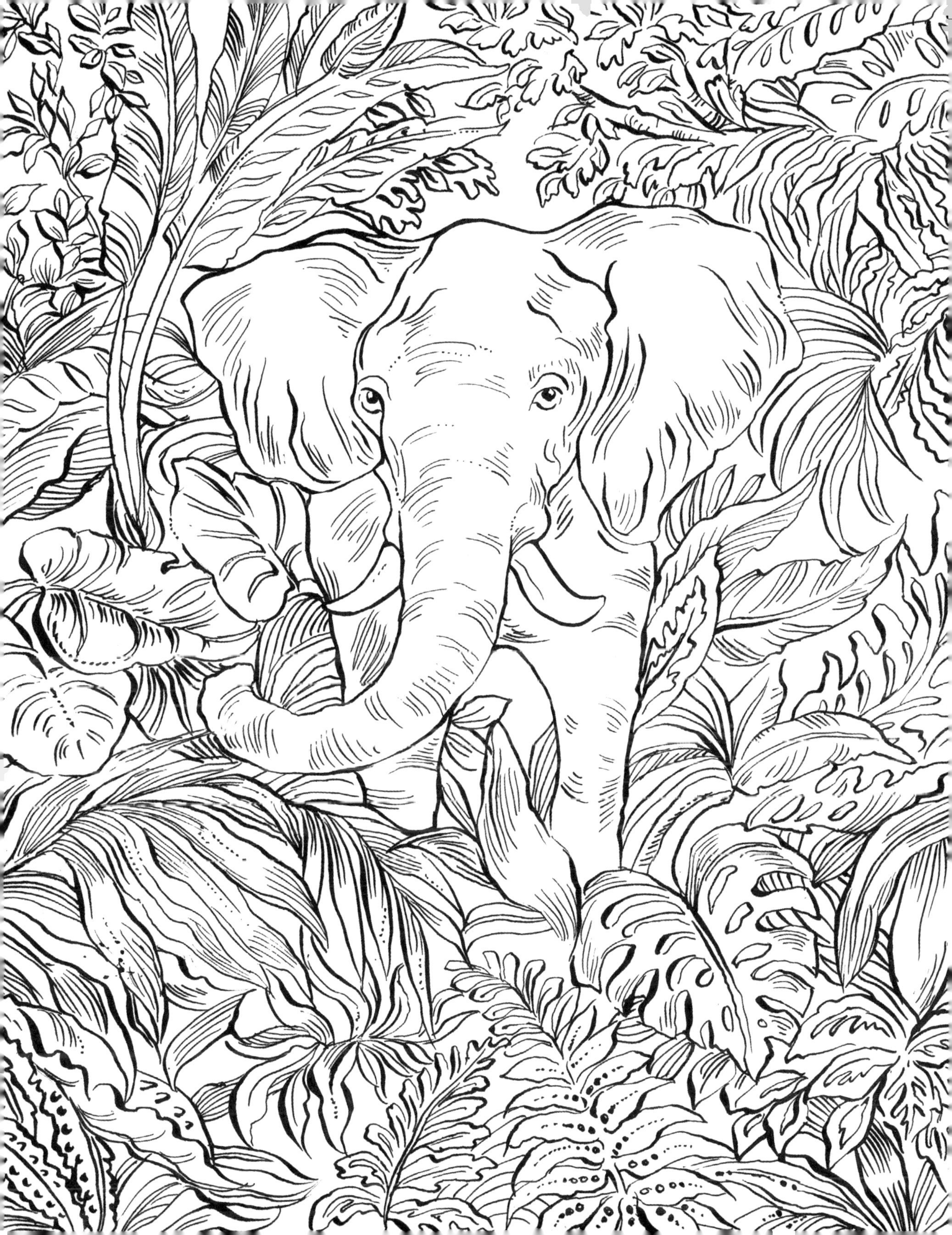

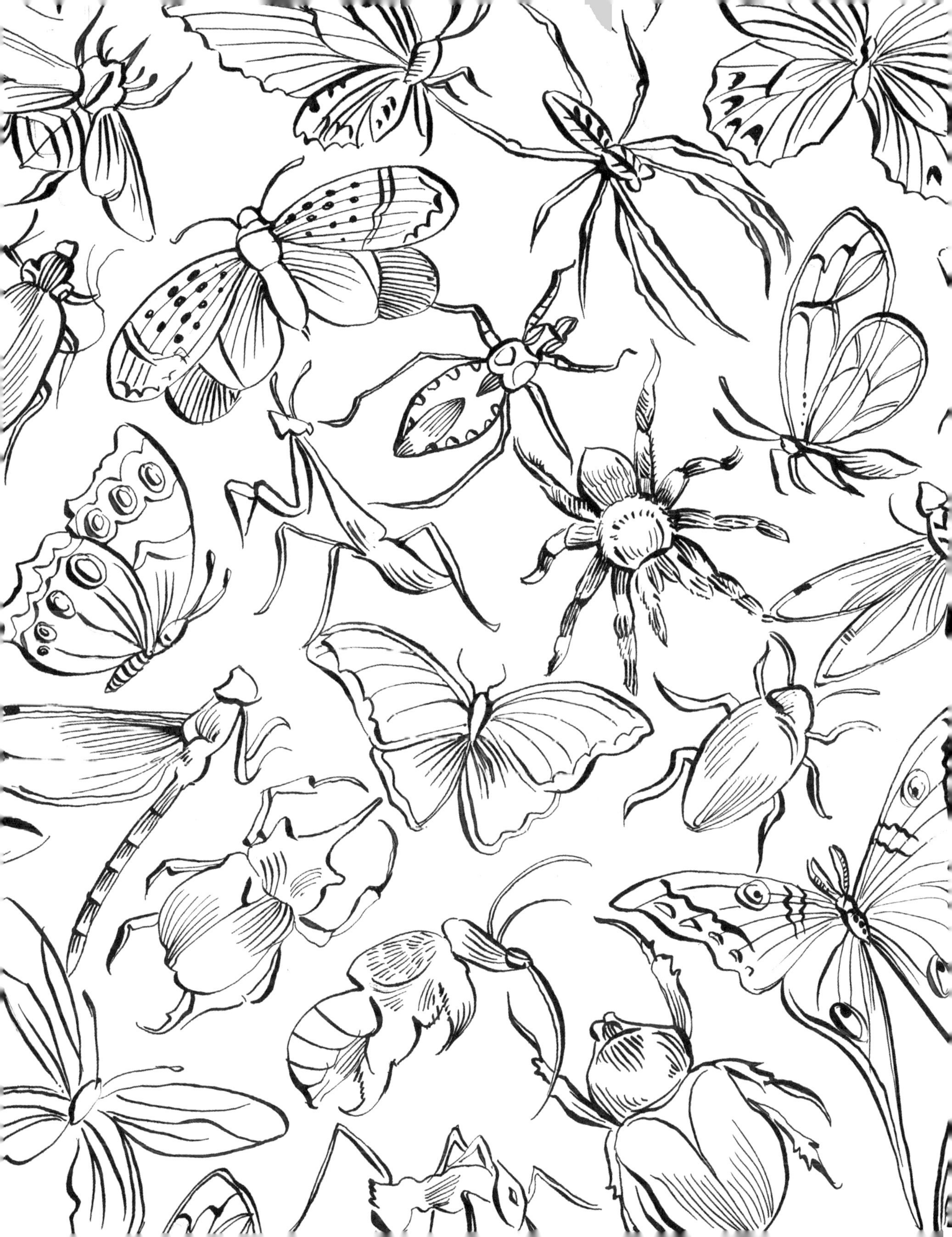

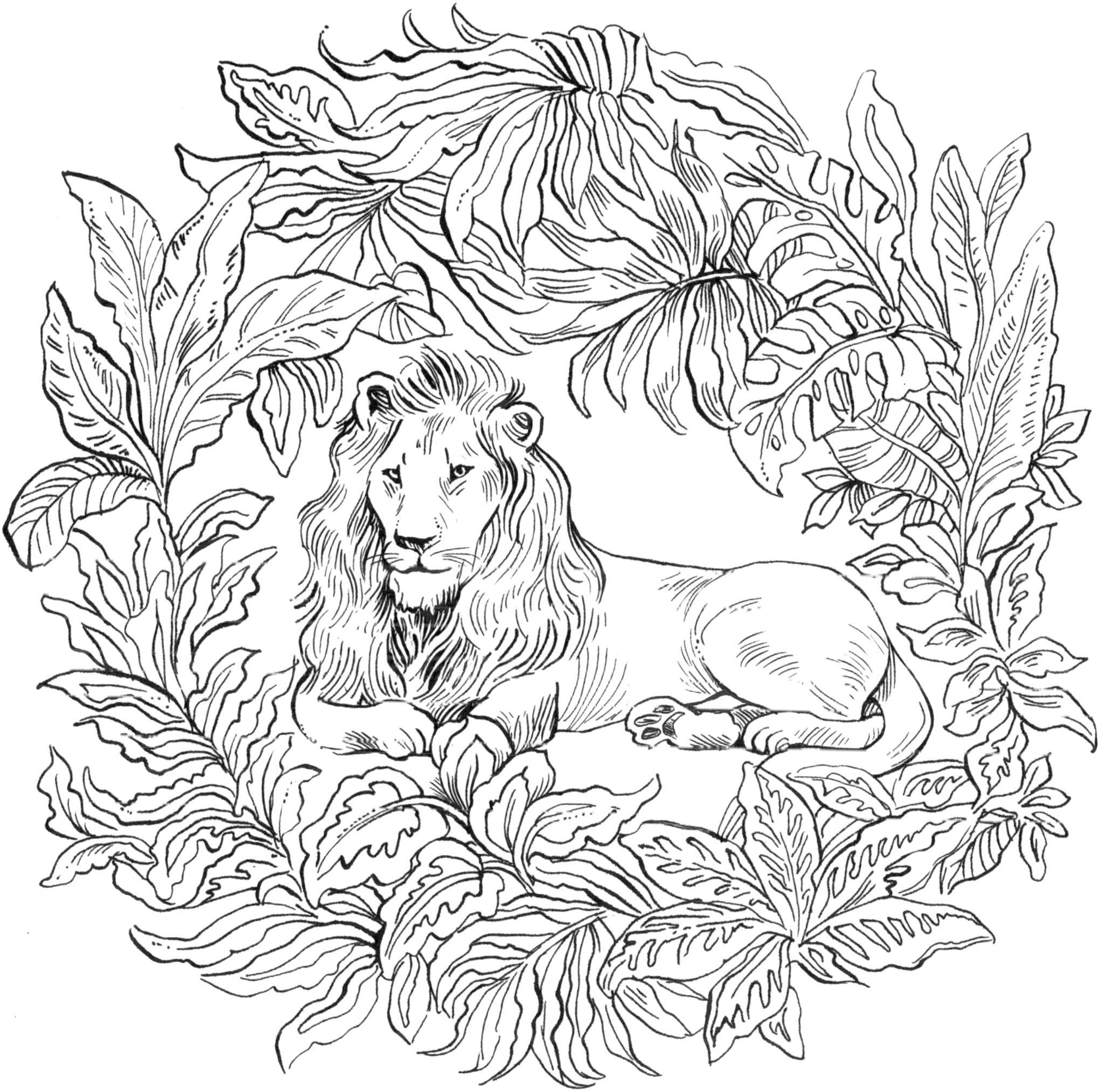

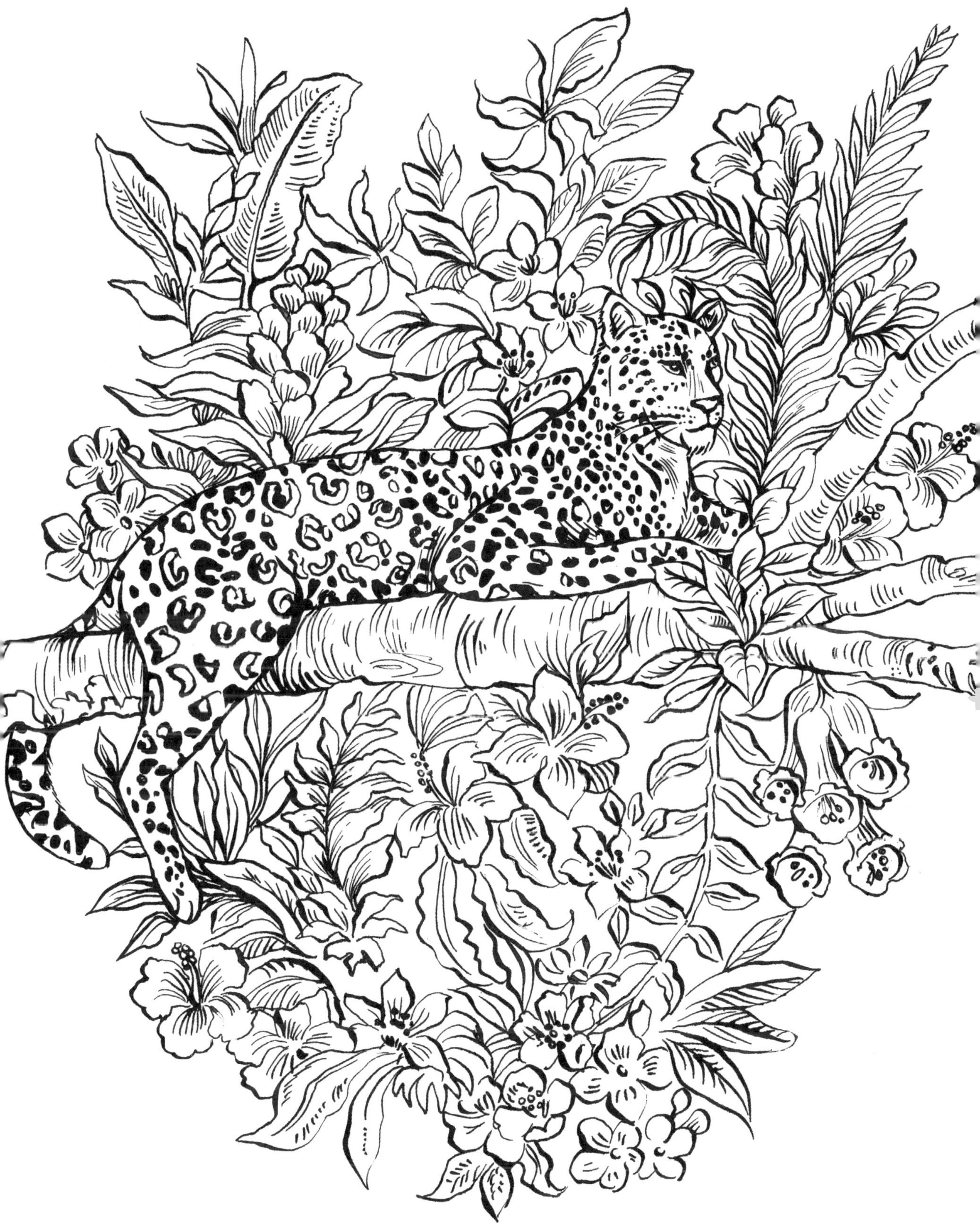

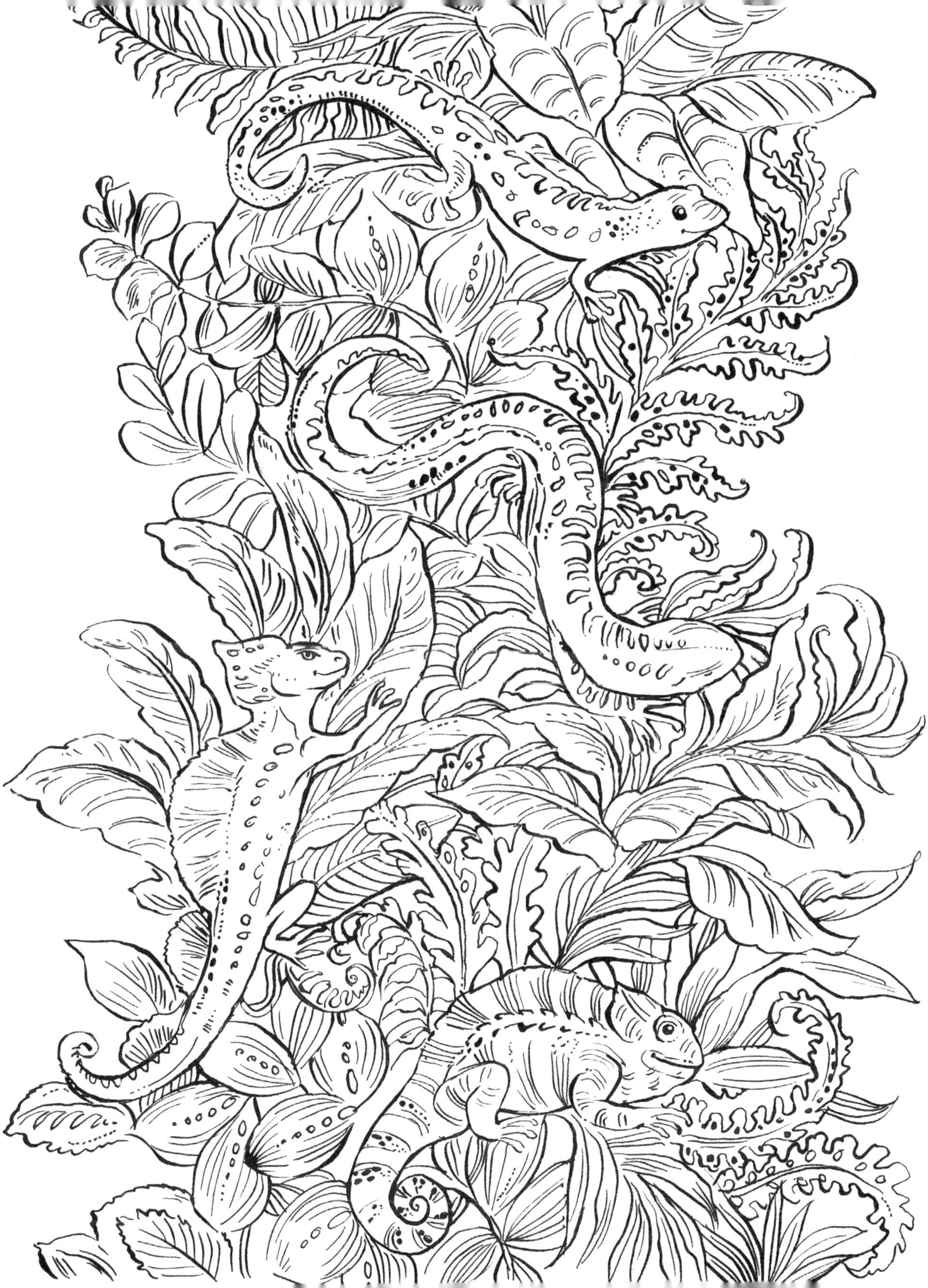

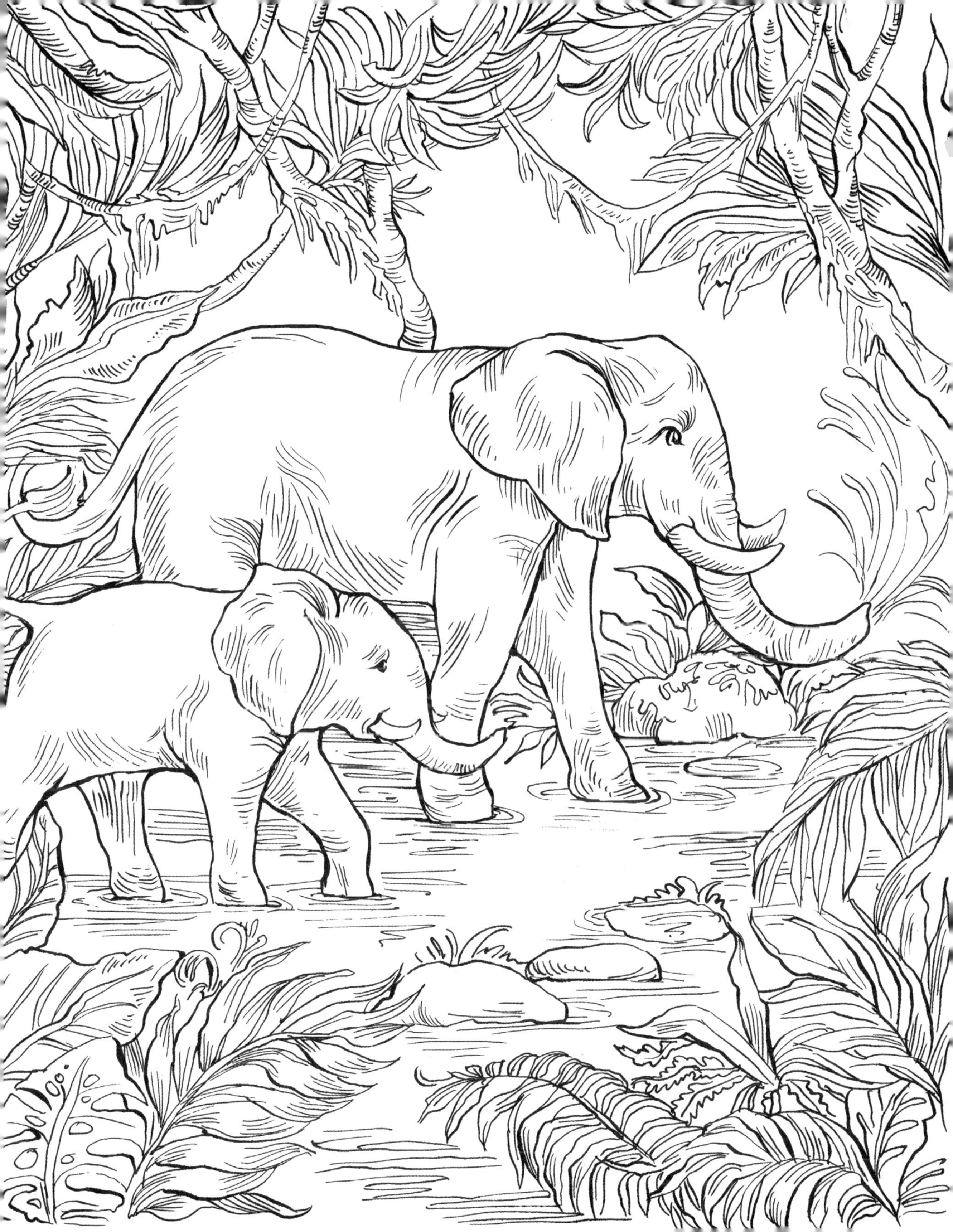

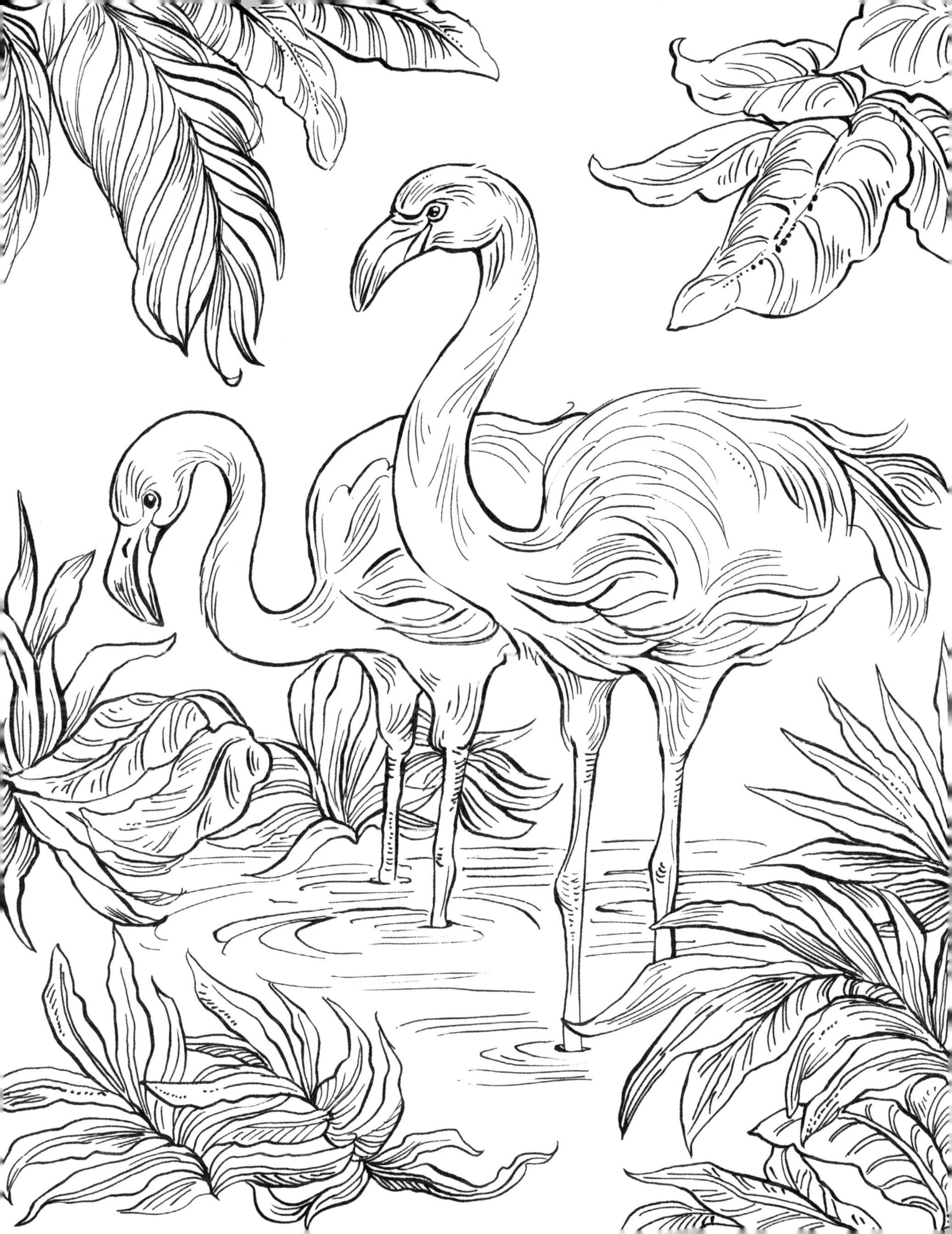

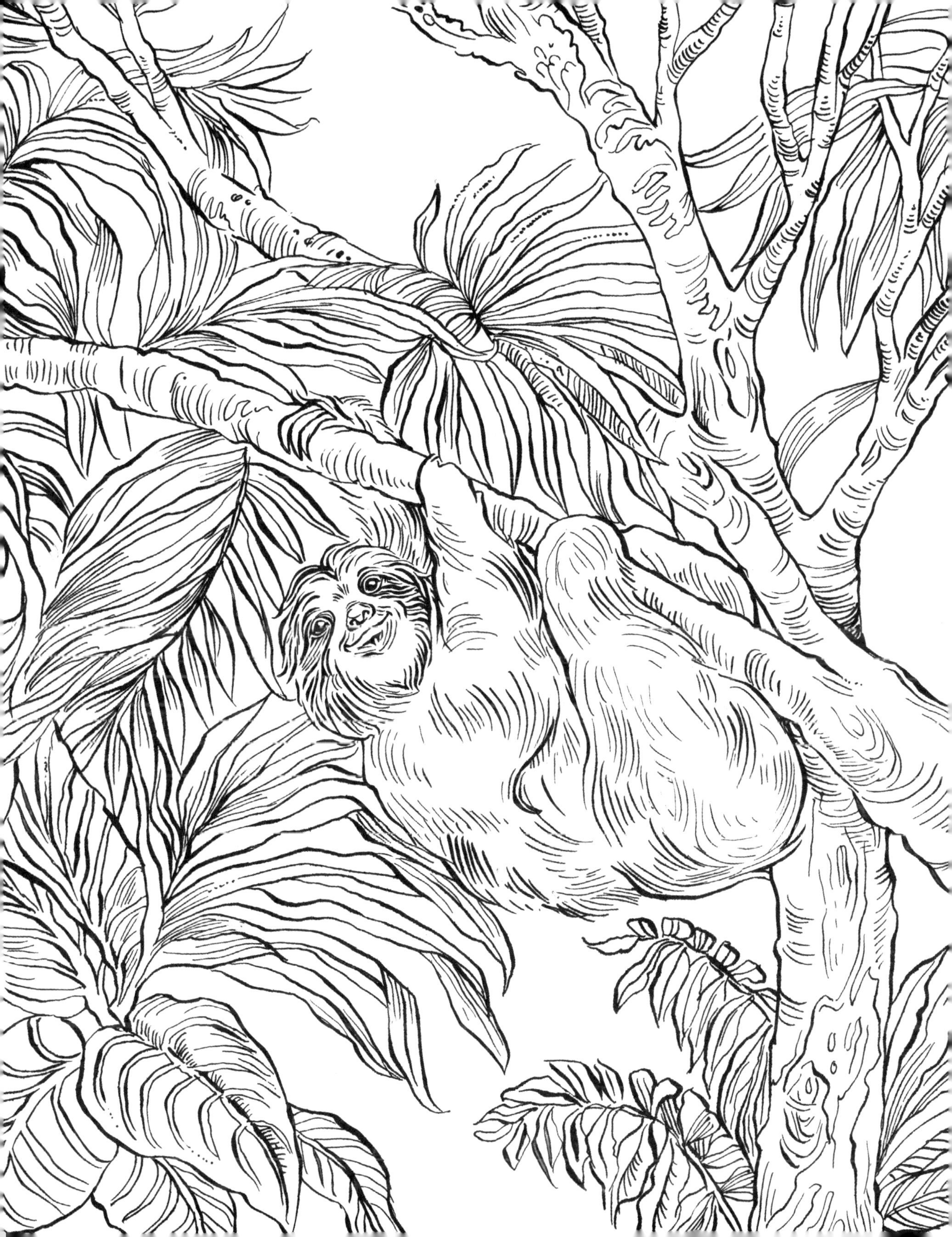

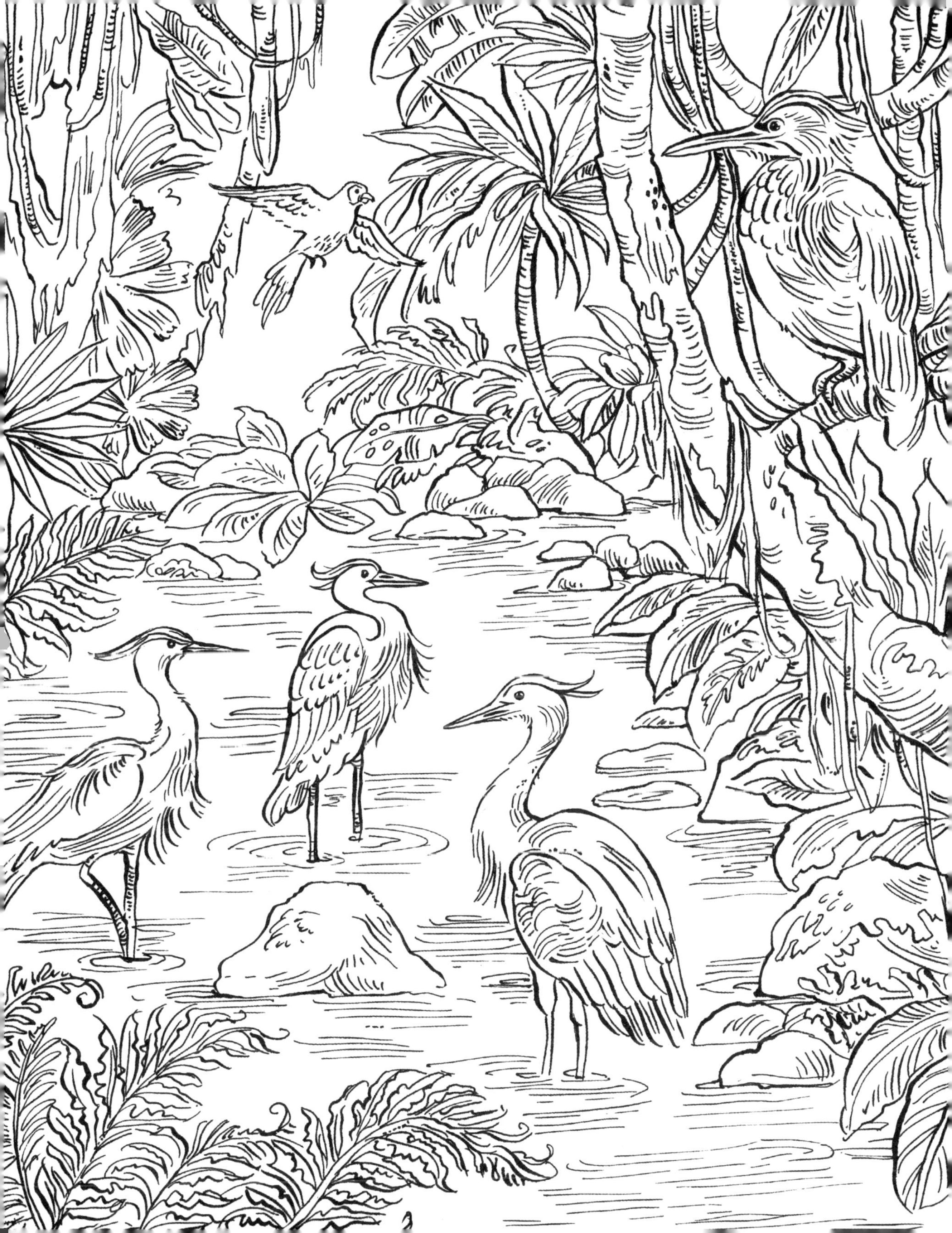

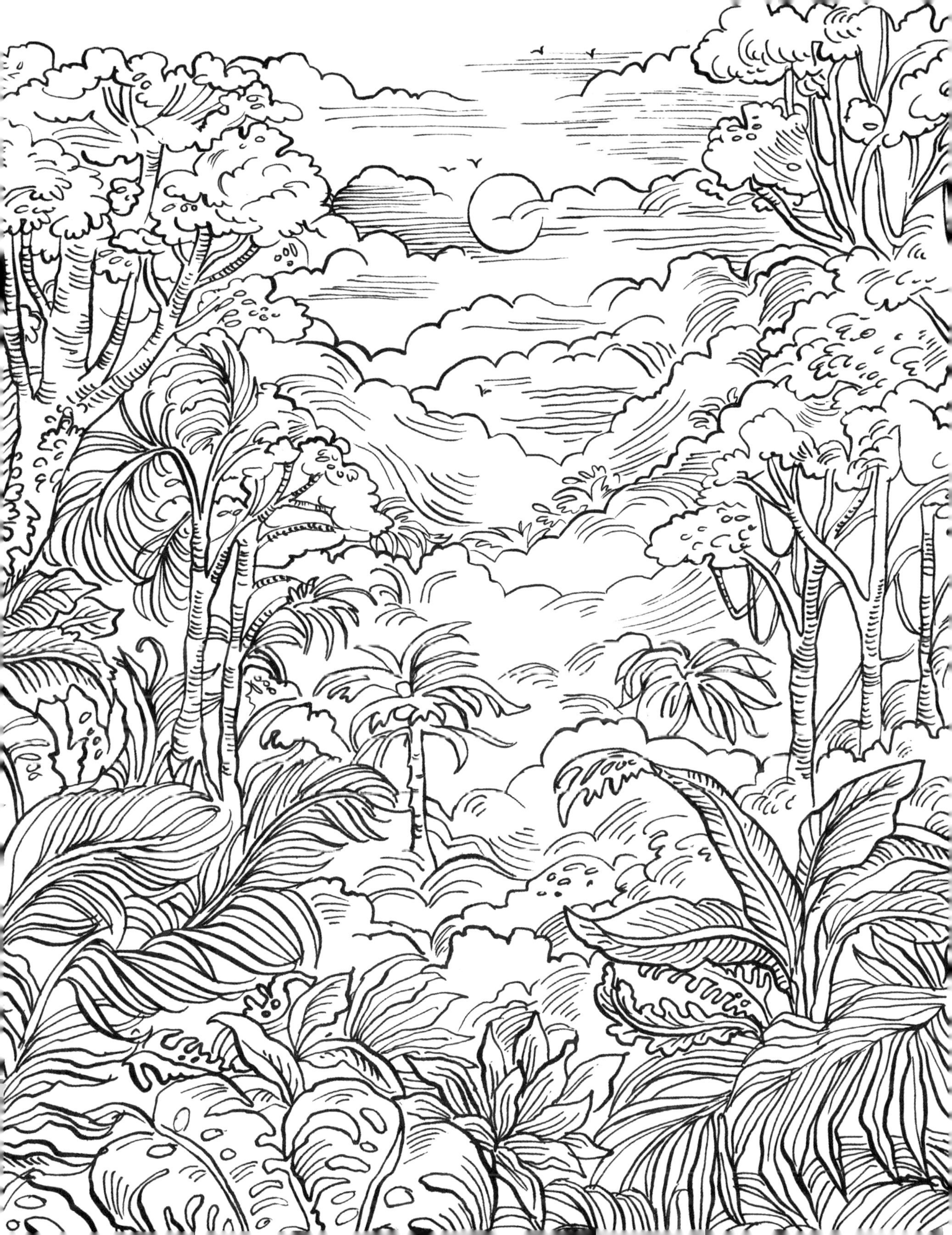

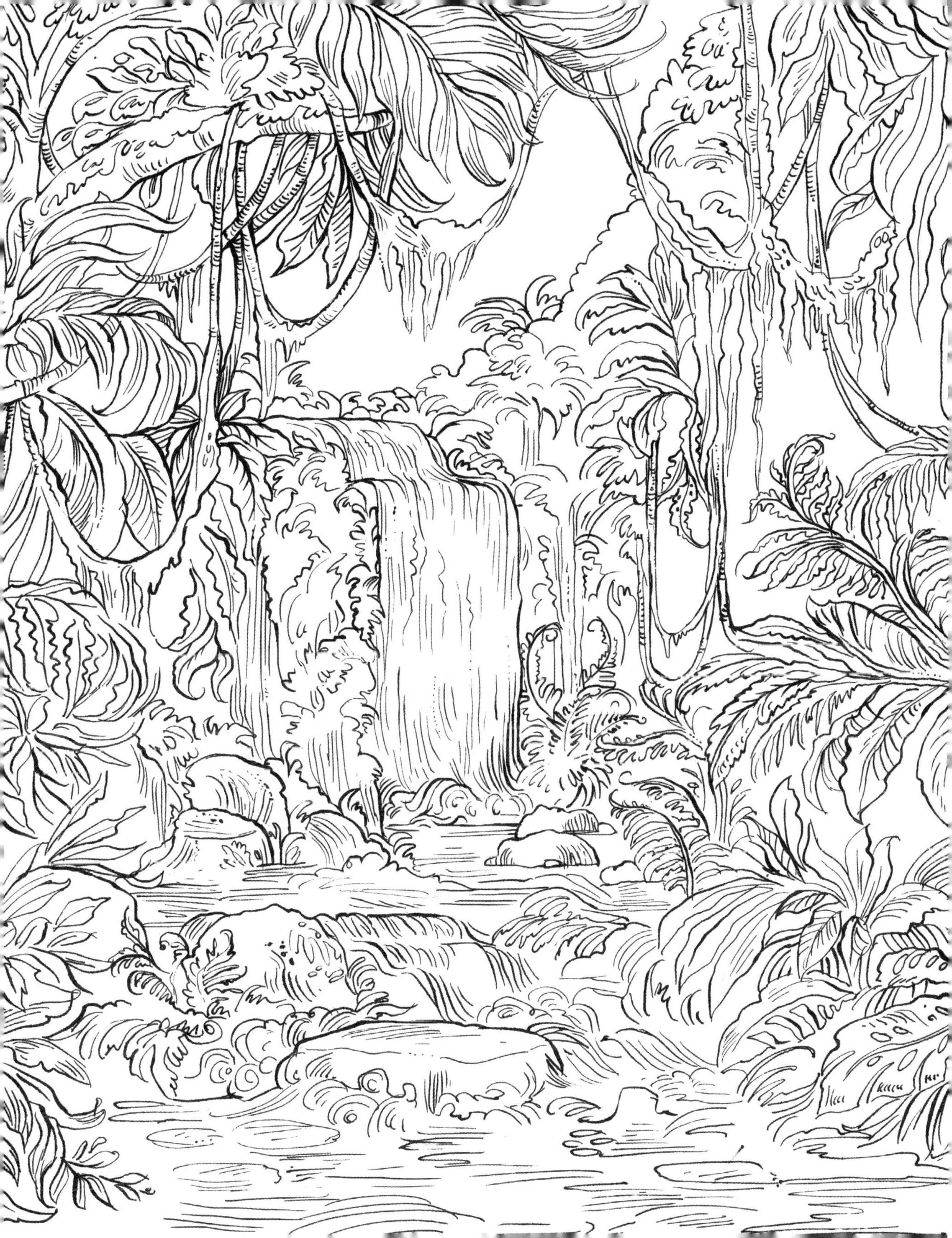

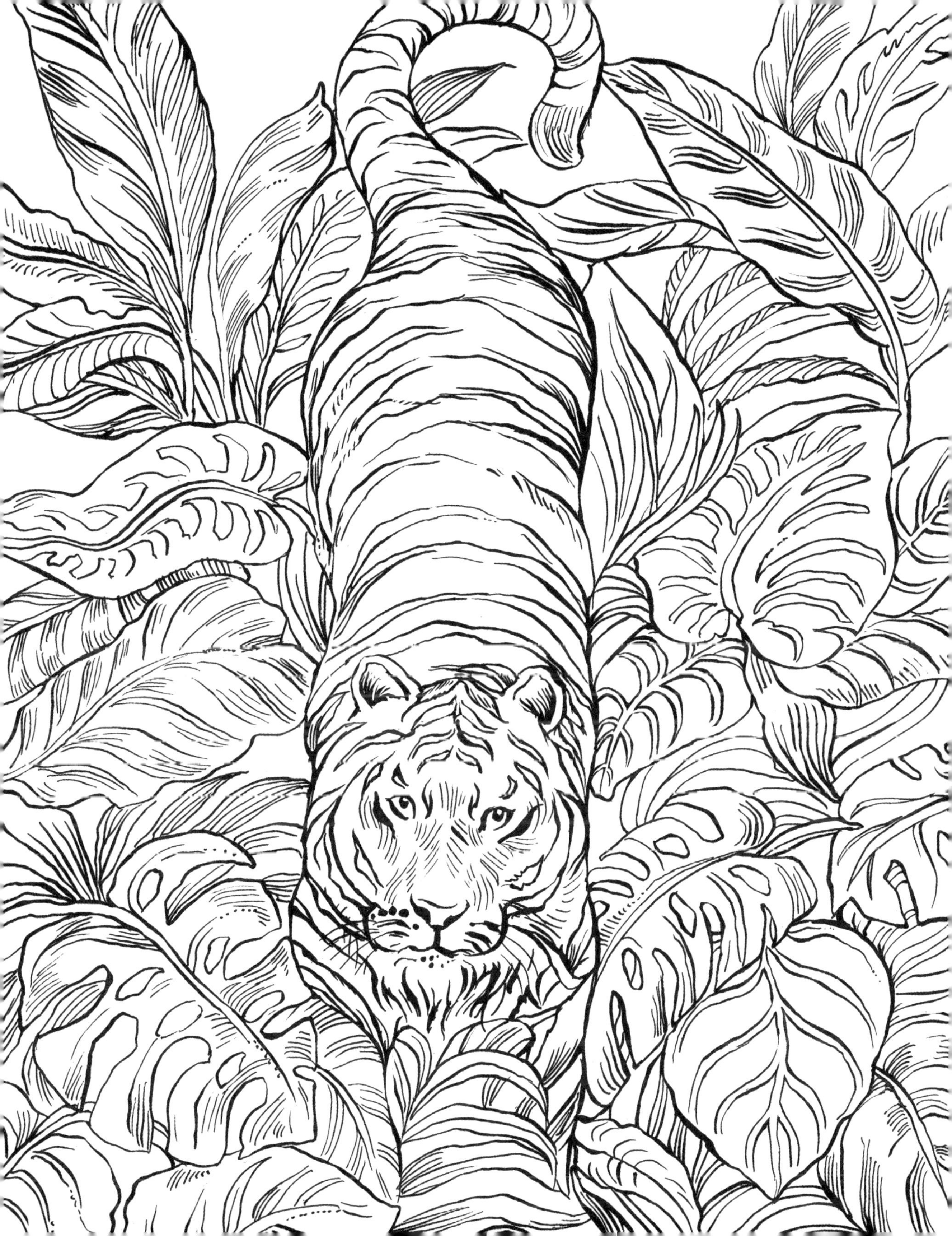

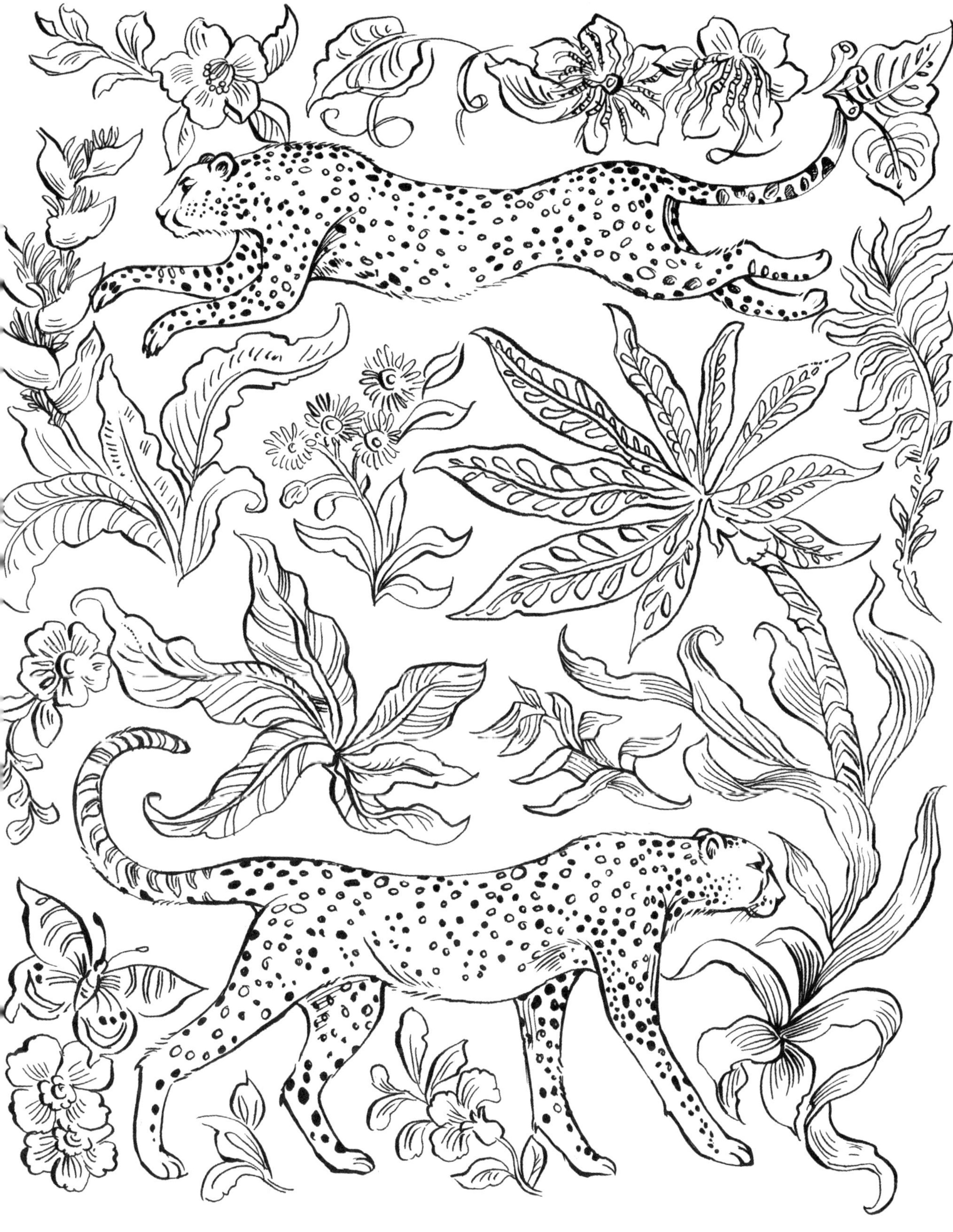

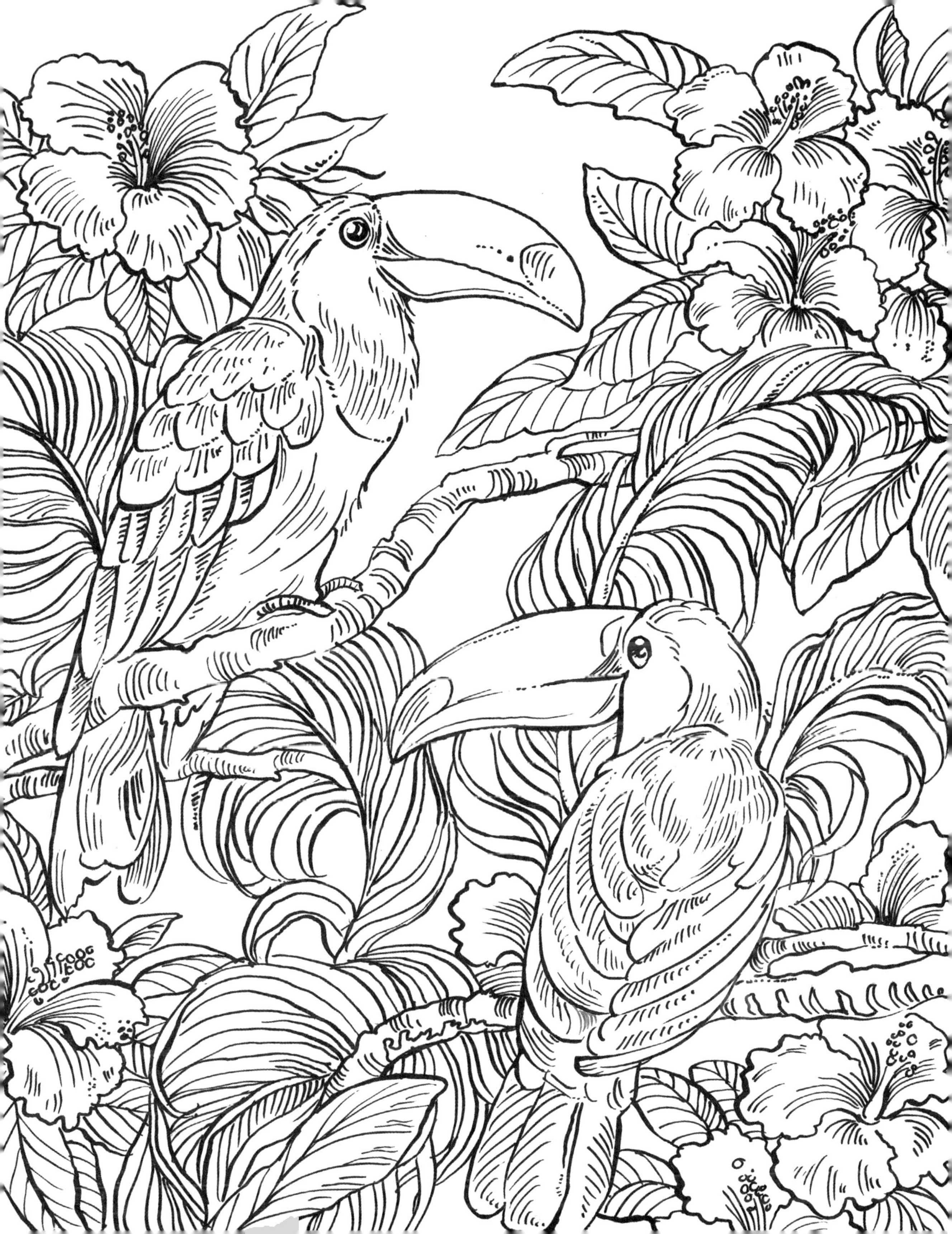

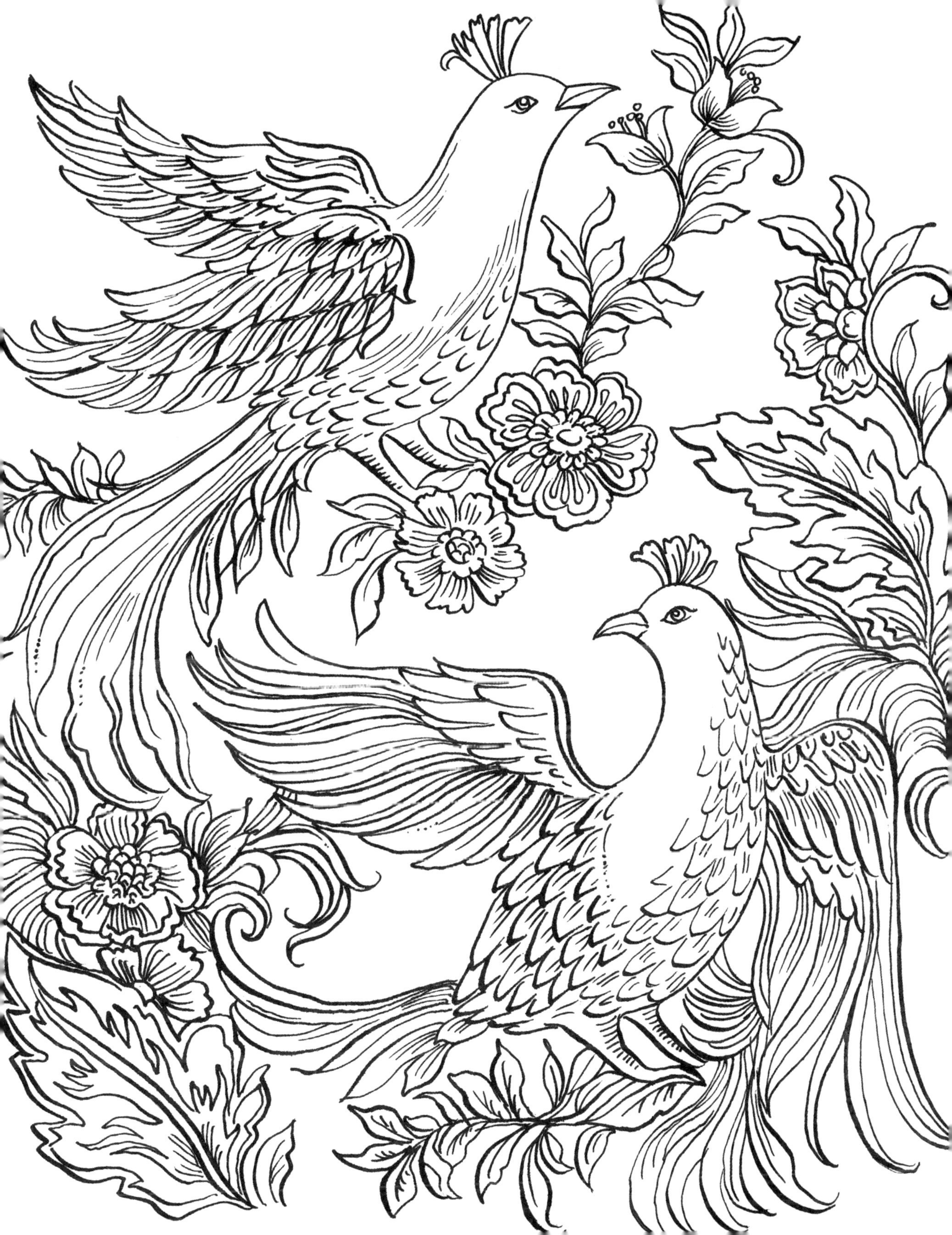

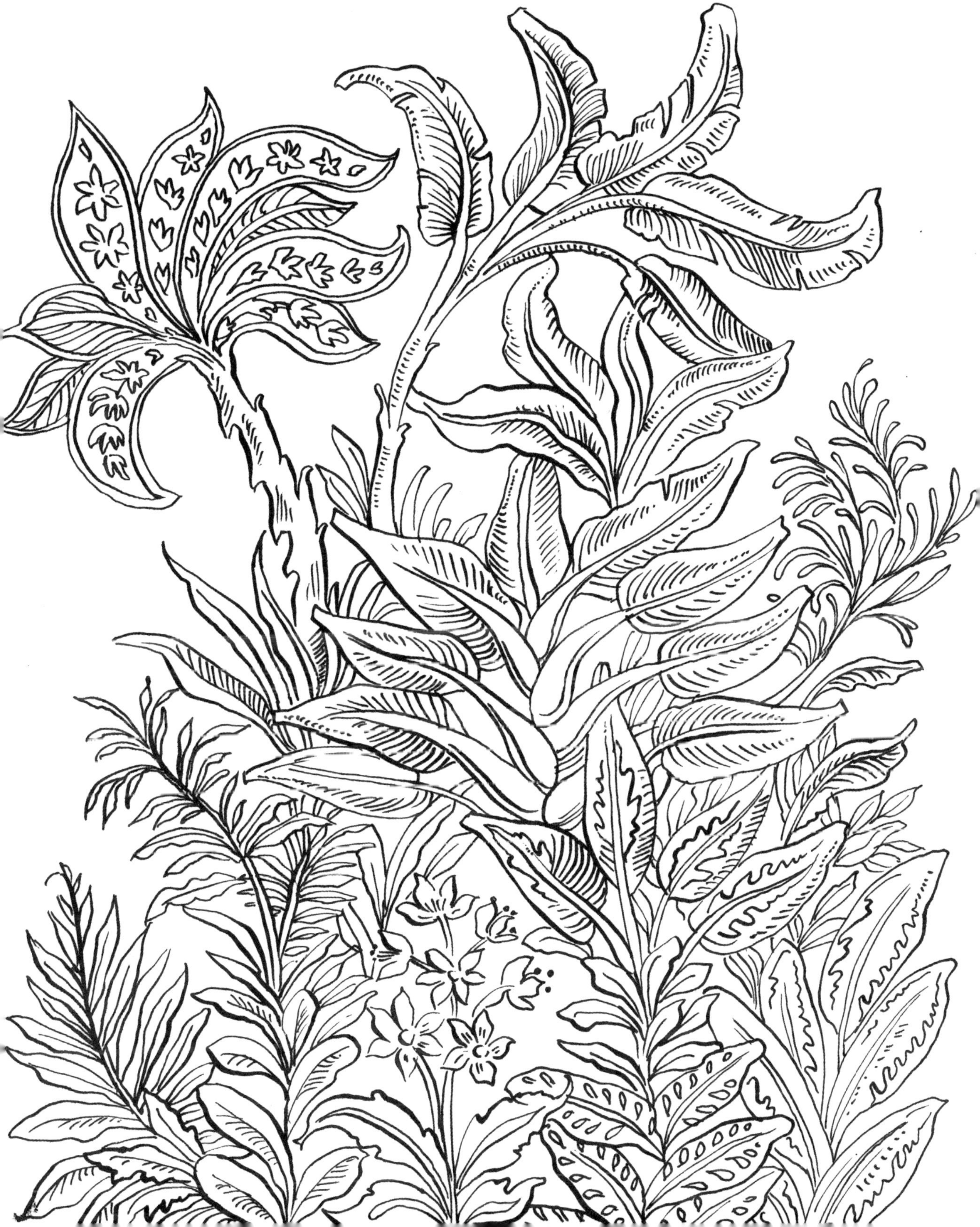

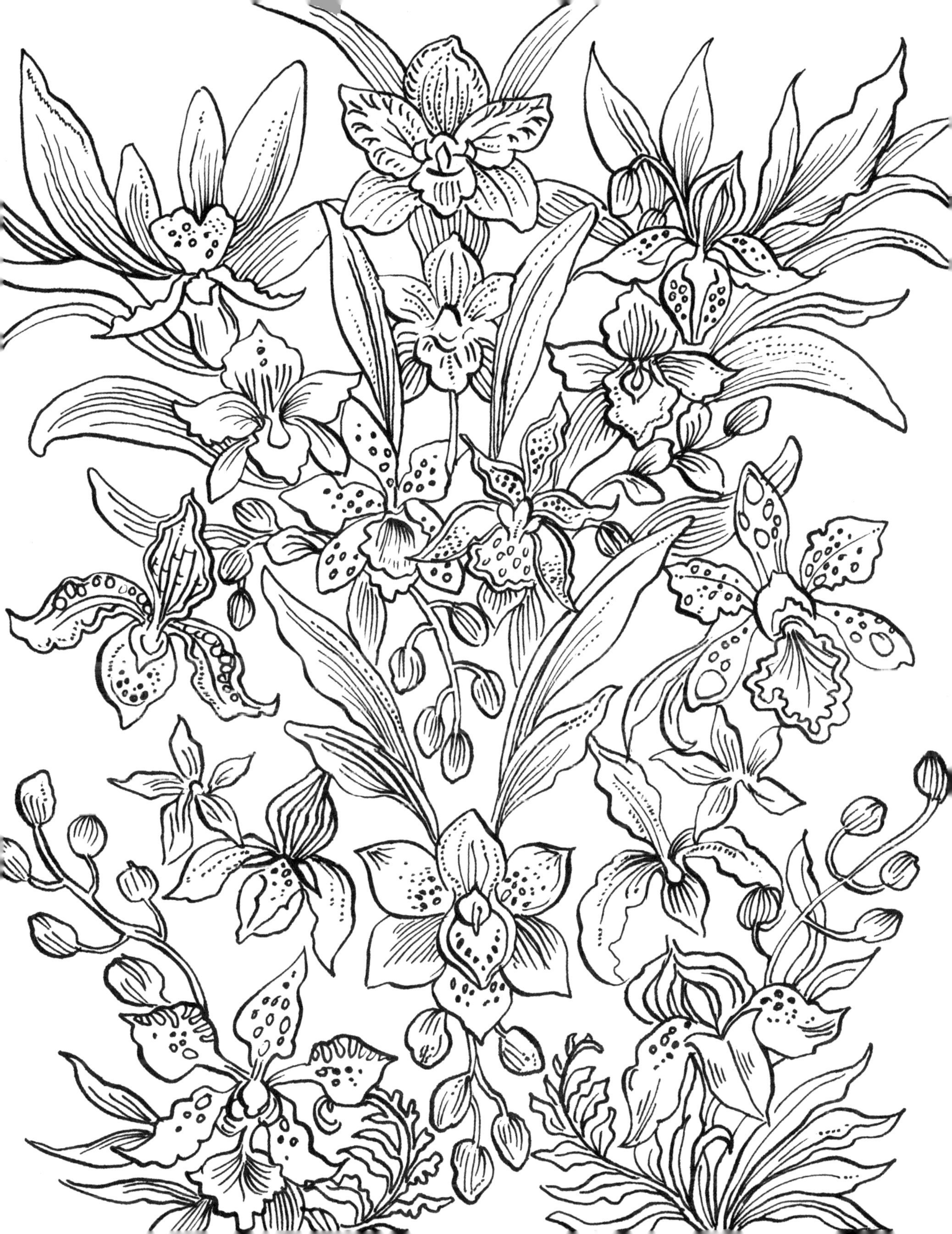

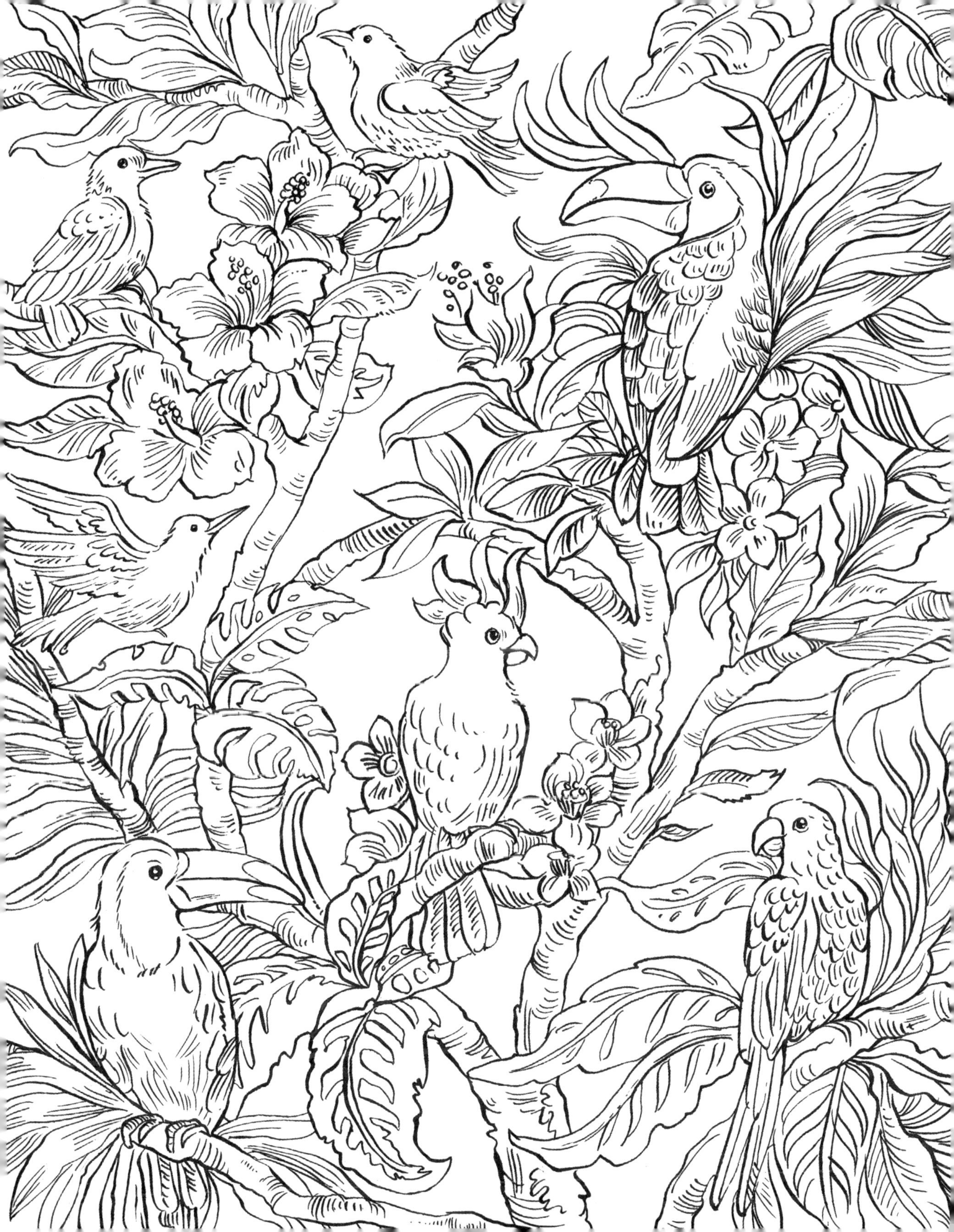

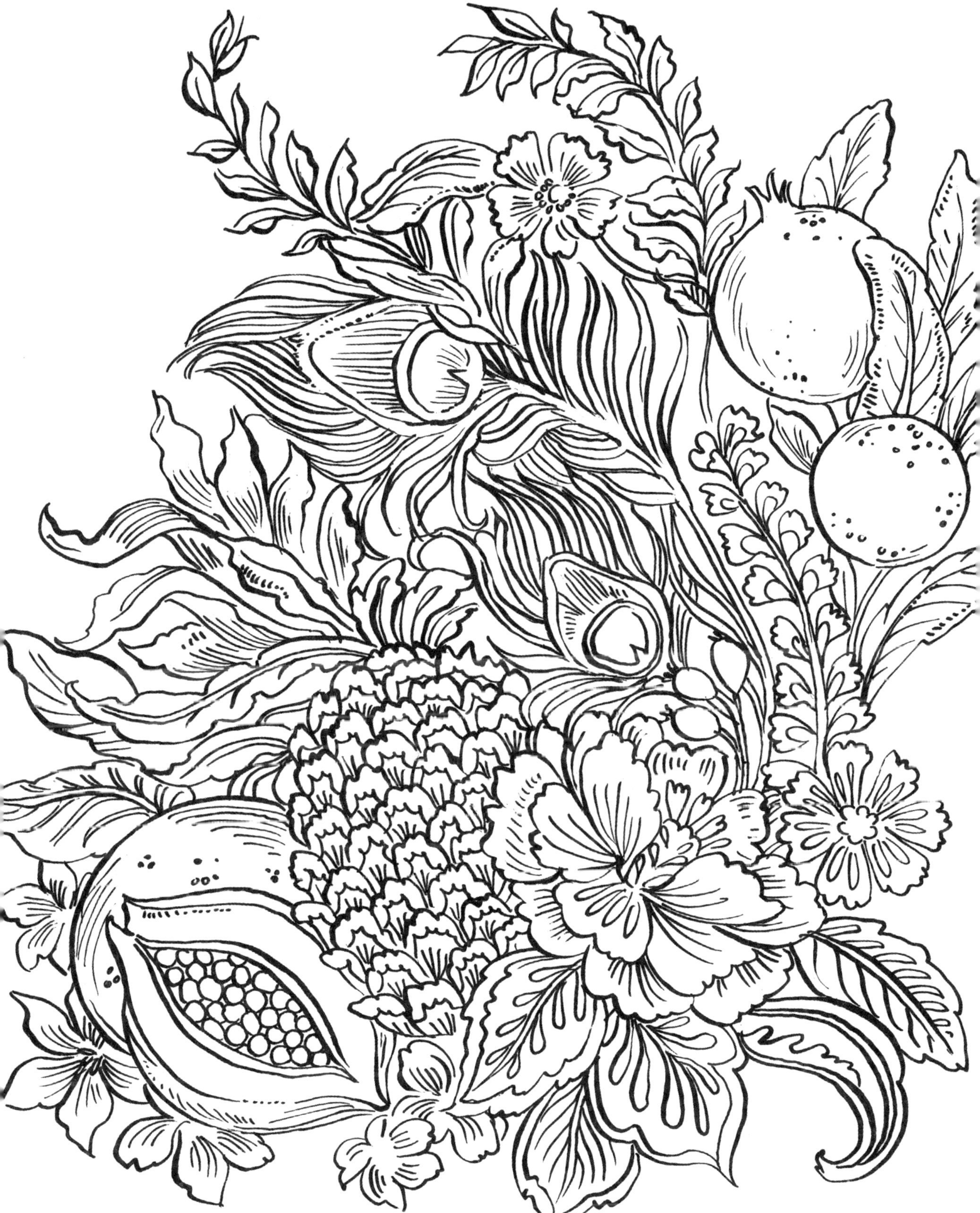

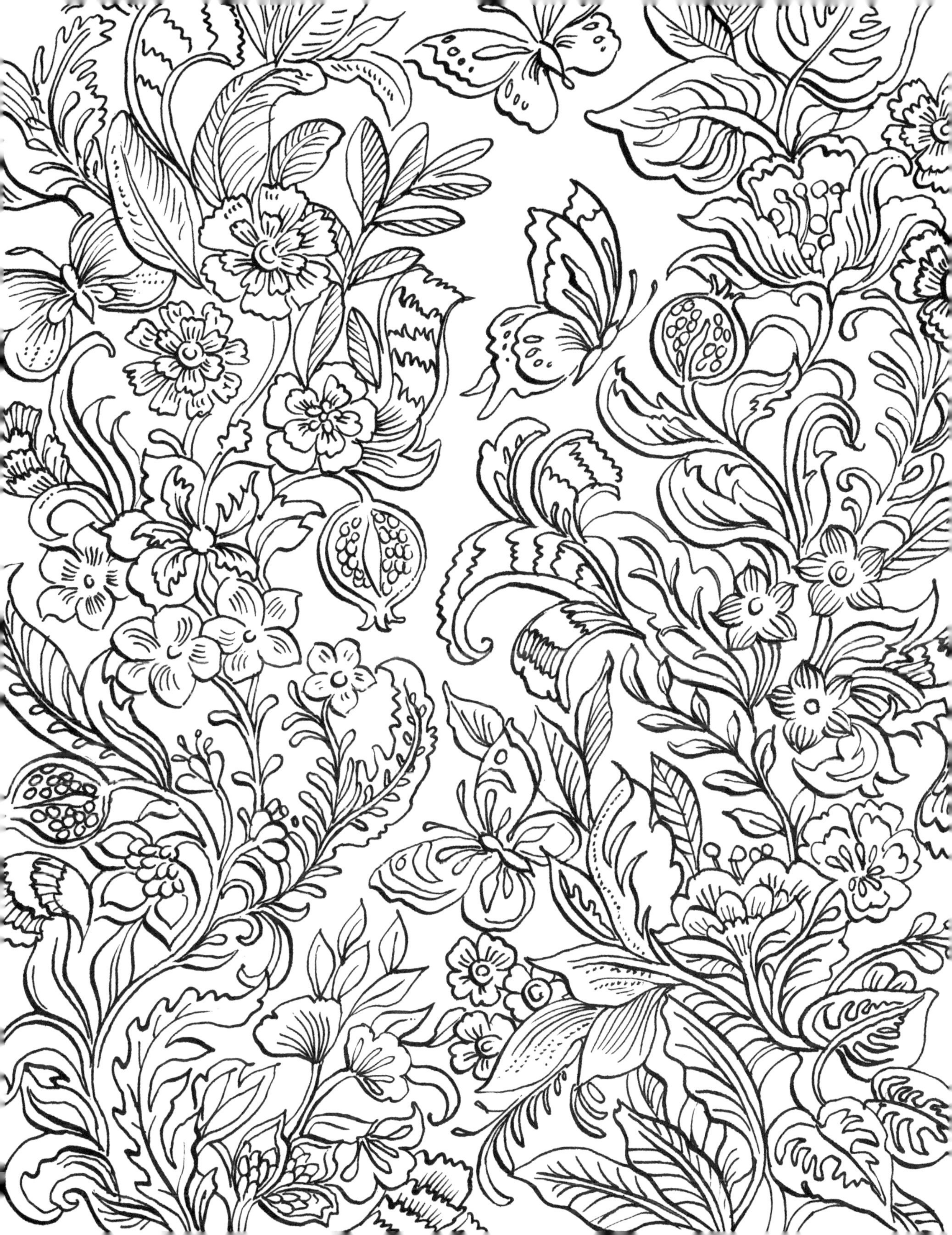

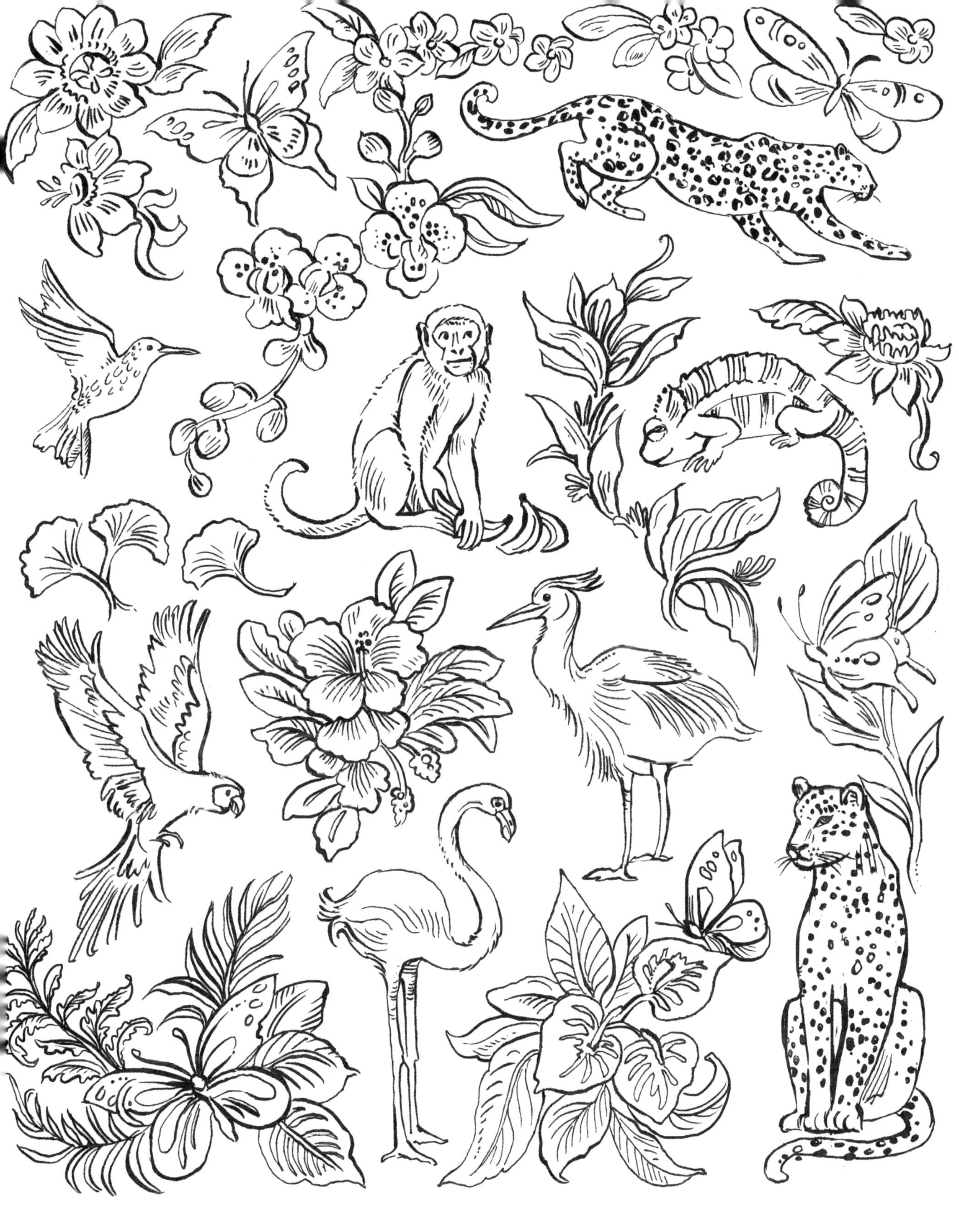

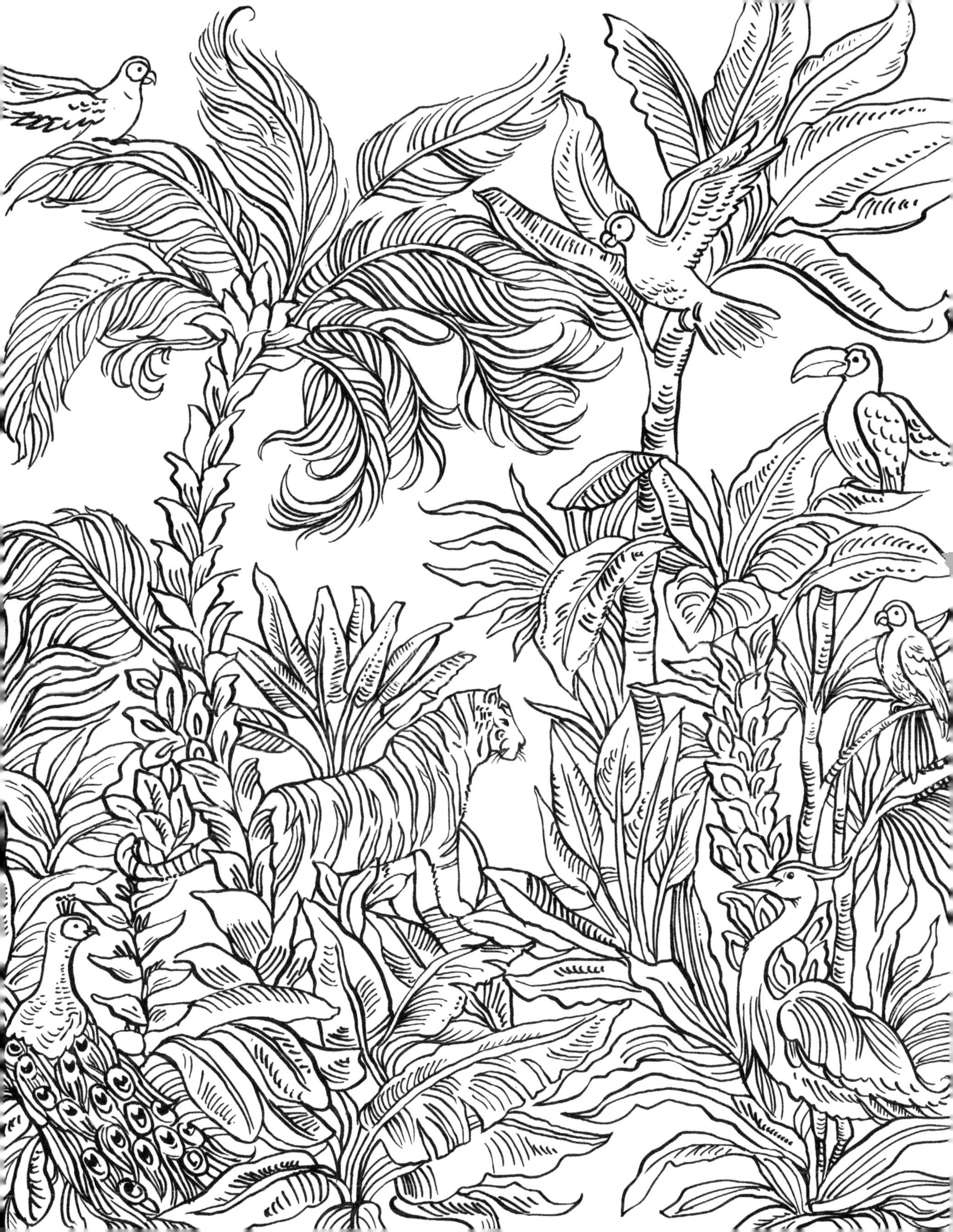

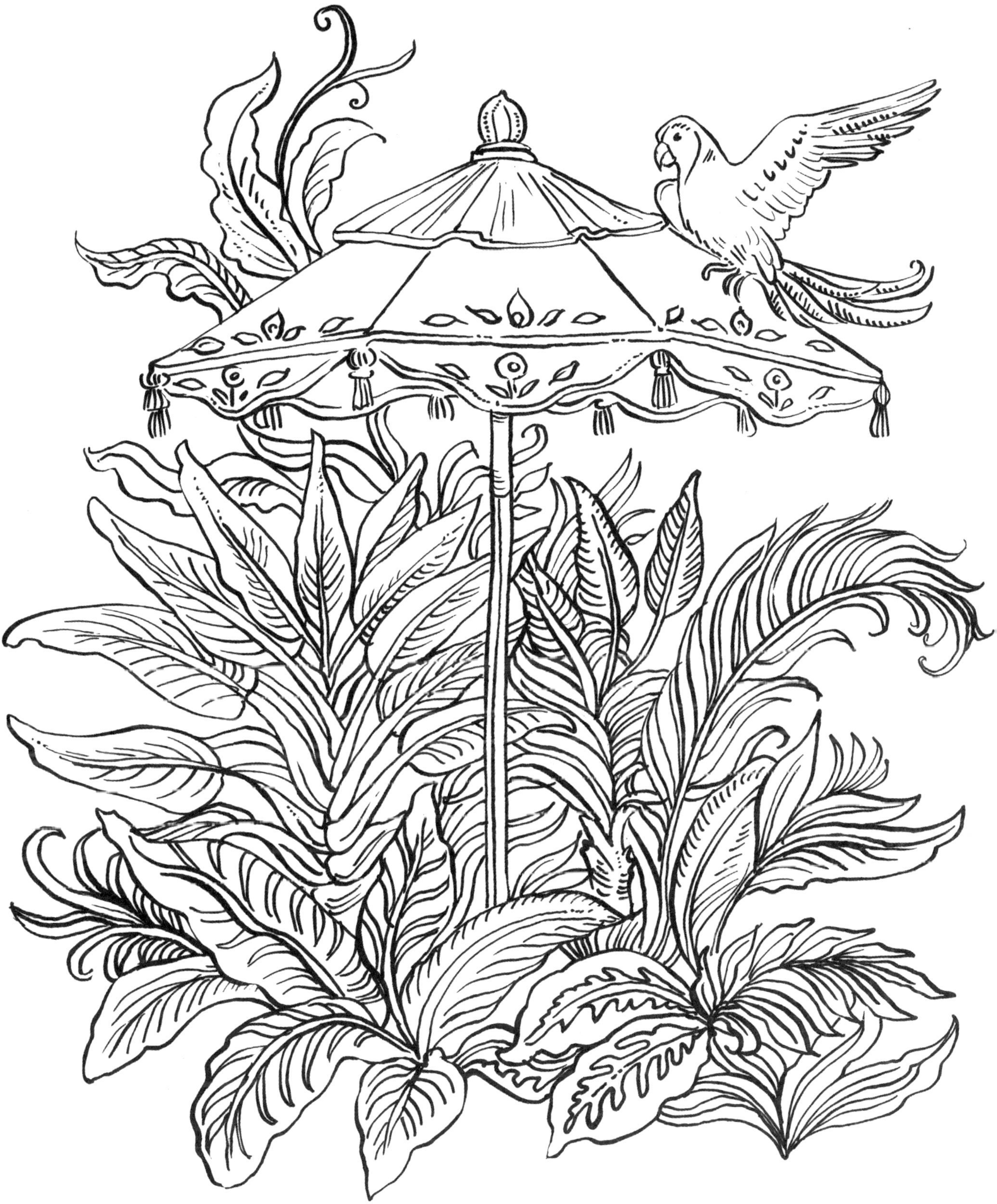

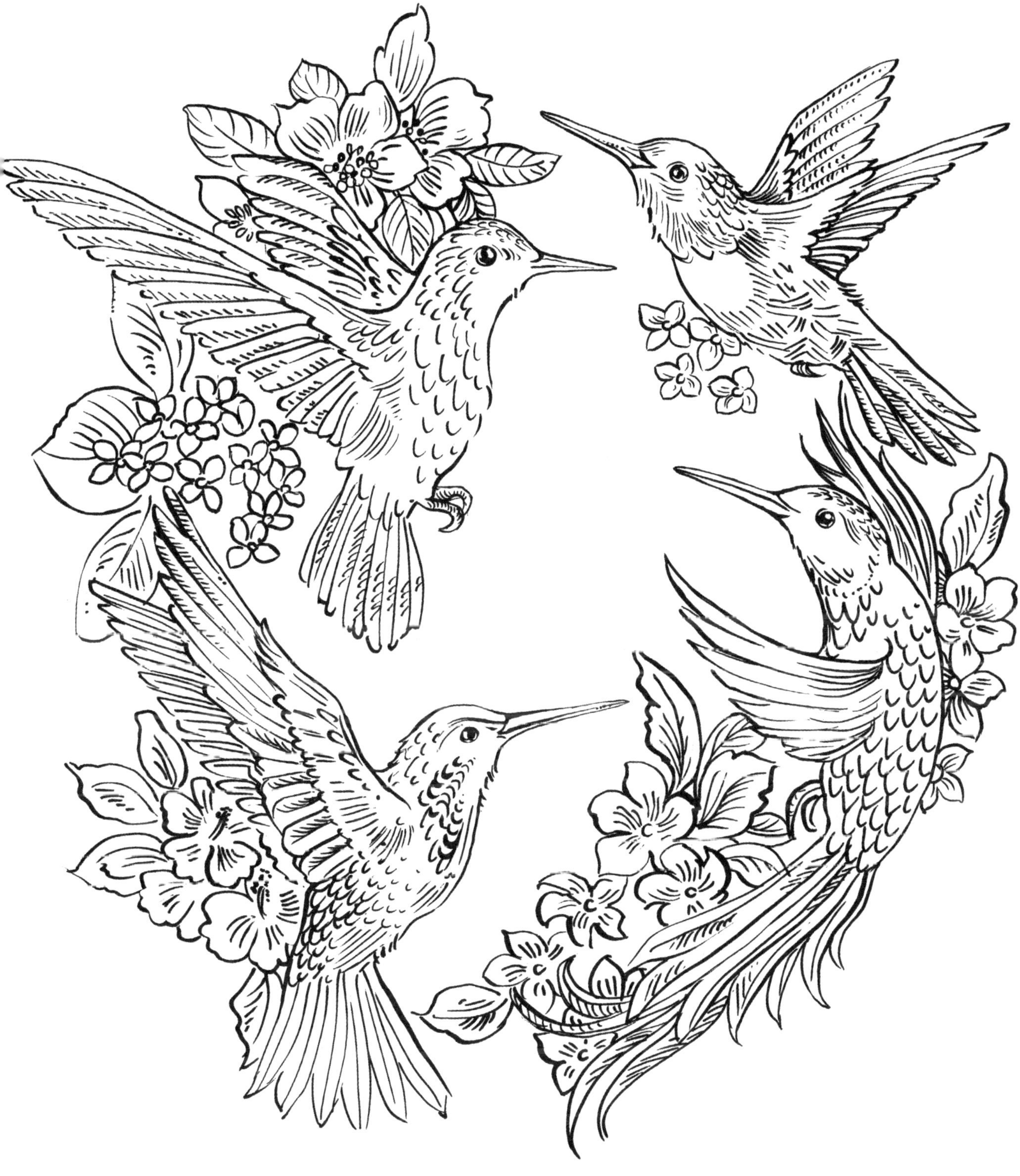

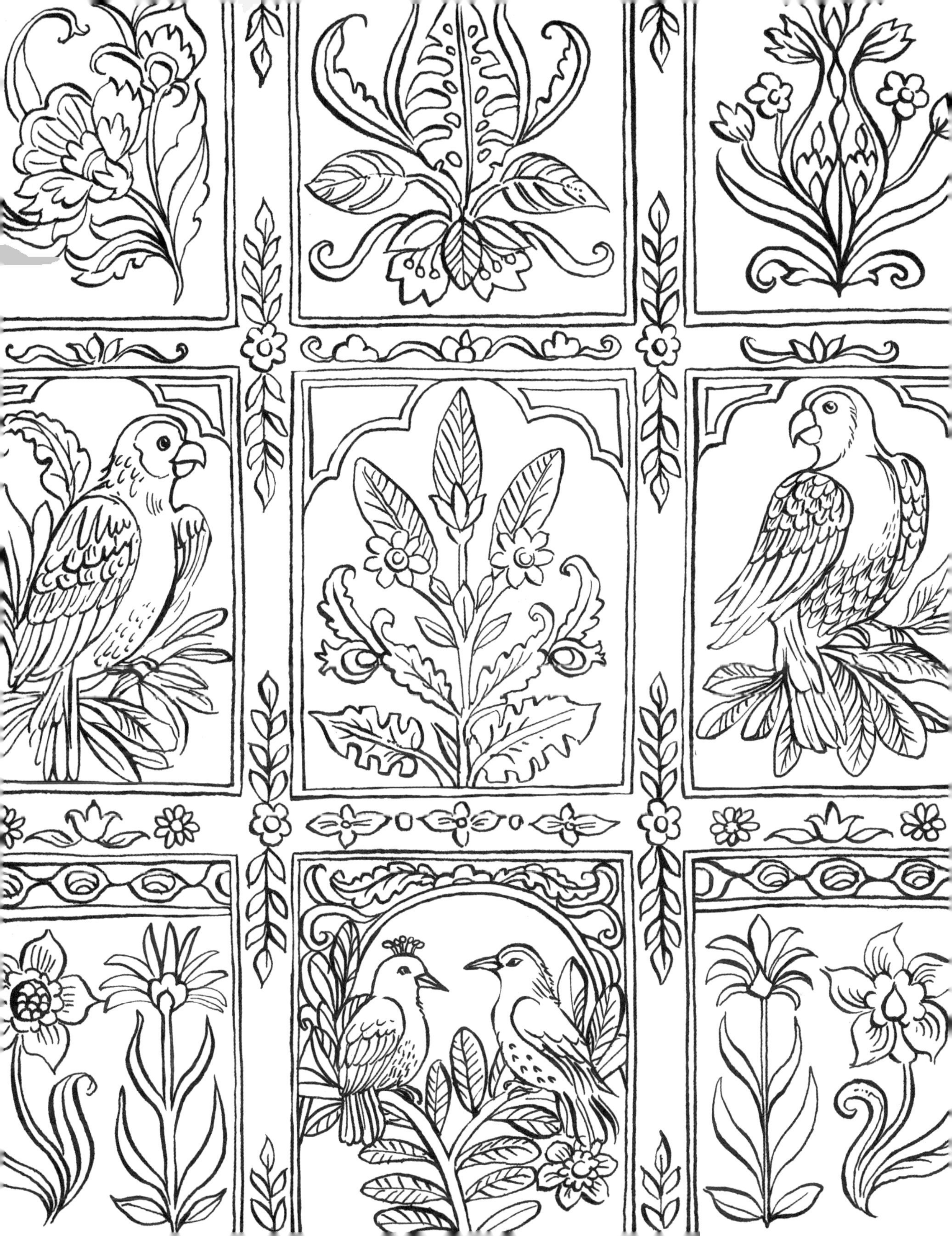